The World of Animals

ANTELOPES

Editor: Winwood Reade

For Charles Pitman

The World of Animals

ANTELOPES

RENNIE BERE

Published simultaneously by
Arco Publishing Company, Inc.
219 PARK AVENUE SOUTH, NEW YORK, N.Y. 10003

and

Arthur Barker Limited
5 WINSLEY STREET LONDON W I

Sources and Acknowledgements

In attempting to review, even superficially, all the world's antelopes I have had to range far beyond my personal experience; this has meant consulting numerous articles, scientific papers and books of reference. Space does not permit a full list but a select bibliography is given later. Many of the articles and papers are to be found in the following journals: *East African Wildlife Journal, Journal of Wildlife Management, Mammalia,* and *Oryx.* Of outstanding importance is *The Past and Present Distribution of some African Ungulates* by Jasmine Sidney (1965), published by the Zoological Society of London. Other authors of papers or articles are: John Blower, Helmut Buechner, P.E.Glover, Ian Grimwood, Bernhard Grzimek, Marthe Kiley-Worthington, H.F.Lamprey, W.Linnard, W.H. Pearsall, Clive Spinage, Lee Talbot, Desmond Vesey-Fitzgerald, and Murray Watson.

The Systematic List which forms an appendix to this book is based on the publications of Allen (1939), Ellerman & Morrison-Scott (1951), Morris (1965), and W.F.H.Ansell's draft revision of the *Artiodactyla.* While preparing the Descriptive Notes I have made considerable use of *Rowland Ward's Records of Big Game*: Tenth Edition (1935), African and Asiatic Sections, by G.Dollman and J.B. Burlace; and Twelfth Edition (1962), by G.A.Best, F.Edmond-Blanc and R.C.Whiting. I am indebted to Mr Gerald Best for permission to do this. I am also grateful to Sandy Field, Chief Warden of the Serengeti National Park in Tanzania, for reading and criticising parts of my text.

RENNIE BERE

Acknowledgements for Illustrations

The author and publishers are indebted to the following for permission to reproduce photographs in this book: Mr T. Angermayer and Bruce Coleman Ltd for the photograph on page 11; Mr D. Bartlett, Armand Denis Productions and Bruce Coleman Ltd for the photographs on pages 10 (*bottom*), 21, 29, 82, 83; Mr N. Bedi and Bruce Coleman Ltd for the photograph on page 7; Miss J. Burton and Bruce Coleman Ltd for the photographs on pages 9 (*top*), 46 (*bottom*), 79, 90; Mr B. Campbell, Armand Denis Productions and Bruce Coleman Ltd for the photographs on pages 28, 85; Mr C. A. W. Guggisberg and Bruce Coleman Ltd for the photographs on pages 31, 33, 47, 89; Mr J. Hanks for the photograph on page 58; Mr E. Hosking for the photograph on page 22 (*bottom*); Mr E. Hosking and Mr G. Mountfort for the photograph on page 22 (*top*); Mr R. Kinne and Bruce Coleman Ltd for the photograph on page 80; Mr N. Myers for the photographs on pages 6, 8, 9 (*bottom*), 10 (*top*), 12, 13, 15, 16, 24, 27, 30 (*top*), 34 and 35, 36, 37, 38, 40 and 41, 42, 45, 48, 52 and 53, 54, 55, 56, 57, 60, 61, 63, 64, 66, 67, 69, 70, 71, 72, 74, 76, 84, 86, 87; Mr J. Savidge for the photograph on page 49; Mr J. Taylor for the photograph on page 78; Tierbilder Okapia for the photograph on page 25; Mr S. Trevor and Bruce Coleman Ltd for the photograph on page 39; Mr R. Wheater for the photographs on pages 14, 30 (*bottom*), 43, 46 (*top*), 62; and Mr J. Whiteman for the photographs on pages 19, 32.

Contents

CHAPTER ONE

Kingdom of the antelopes

A great herd of wildebeest grazes placidly on the wide open Serengeti plains. Gazelles pick their dainty way across the arid steppe-land of the Horn of Africa, identical with animals carved in ivory at Thebes during the eighteenth Egyptian dynasty. The few oryx still left in Saudi Arabia feed on the sparse vegetation of the Rub-al-khali desert. Tiny grizzled dikdik peer timidly from a thicket in the African bush. A giant eland grazes in the lightly wooded savanna of the Congo-Uganda borderland. Bushbuck and duikers move silently through the equatorial forests. Impala slip in and out of the acacia scrub with a grace unsurpassed by any living land animal. A kudu bull lays his great horns along his back as he disappears into the undergrowth of the Kruger National Park. Uganda kob walk in line to a water-hole in the Lake George flats. These are the antelopes: one of the Old World's largest, most diverse and widely distributed groups of animals.

'Antelope' is not a scientific term, but it describes a group of cloven-hoofed ruminants that are quite unmistakable. The word is derived from the Greek *antholops*, meaning 'brightness of eye' – *anthos*, 'flower' or 'brightness' and *ops*, 'eye' – and was first used of a semi-mythical creature which lived on the banks of the Euphrates. *Antholops*, or its Coptic equivalent *pantholops*, was also used of the legendary unicorn whose most probable origin is the Arabian oryx which can look one-horned when seen in profile. Evidently the most striking feature of these animals was considered to be their eyes as this theme reappears in *dorcas* (from *derkomai*, 'I see clearly') which both Greeks and Romans used for the gazelles ('gazelle' itself

Indian Blackbuck: the word 'antelope' was first used for the graceful Indian Blackbuck

OPPOSITE: Bohor Reedbuck: a typical antelope showing the large eyes, sensitive nose and ears, and permanent unbranched horns

7

Bull Eland with Wildebeest and zebra in the Ngorongoro Crater: even-toed and odd-toed ungulates together

Young Guenther's Dikdik: the eyes are a striking feature of all antelopes

derives from the Arabic *ghazal*, meaning 'bright-eyed'). In English the word 'antelope' was first used for the graceful Indian blackbuck. The French naturalist Buffon (1707–88) retained this usage, but the German naturalist Pallas (1741–1811) extended the name to the whole group of which the blackbuck forms a part. At that time only sixteen species were recognized; today the figure is eighty-five.

The antelopes are members of the mammalian order of even-toed ungulates whose diagnostic feature is that the axis of the foot passes between the third and fourth digits. Within that order, they are part of the great *Bovidae* family of hollow-horned ruminants which also includes the buffaloes, bison, cattle, sheep and goats. Lacking an exact scientific definition, antelopes are best described simply as the more delicate and slender-built animals in this family. They have elongated skulls and the typical *Bovidae* tooth-structure with three pairs of incisors in the lower jaw – these are flattened and tend to project forward – but none in the upper jaw. This means that grass must either be plucked with the tongue or pulled with the lower teeth and then cut against the pad of the upper jaw by means of a slight jerk of the head; very tender shoots are sometimes nipped off with the lips. Large cheek-teeth, usually high-crowned and separated from the incisors by a characteristic gap, are present in both jaws and are needed to grind up all the fibrous food consumed.

Deer (*Cervidae*), although similar in many respects, are not antelopes. Both are ruminants with complicated four-chambered stomachs: they chew the cud to make possible the digestion of the vast quantity of vegetable matter consumed. But deer have antlers, usually branched, which are shed and renewed annually. Antelopes have permanent, hollow and unbranched horns supported by bony cores projecting from the skull. This is the most obvious difference between them.

The eyes of antelopes and other ungulates are remarkable. These protrude from the head where the lateral and frontal surfaces join. There is a zone of high sensitivity in the retina corresponding with an elongated pupil. When the eyes rotate in their orbits the pupils remain horizontal. Without moving its head, an antelope can see the whole of a surrounding plain. In fact, most of the more obvious antelope characteristics suggest adaptation to an open habitat: large light-gathering eyes for seeing enemies at a distance and big mobile ears for catching distant sounds; highly sensitive nostrils with enormous smelling organs spread out over the thin bones of the nose; and limbs that are superbly efficient. All the early antelopes seem to have been animals of the plains and steppes. Modern forest dwellers evolved from creatures which retreated into the forests under pressure of predation and the demands of survival. Adapting themselves to their new surroundings with comparatively little change, these have remained much closer to their extinct ancestors than the antelopes living in open country where competition has been fiercer.

Dispersal of the mammals began 70,000,000 years ago when the great reptiles became extinct. As new mammalian killers appeared, the herbivorous animals upon which they preyed had to develop new defences. An ability to escape became the most vital attribute of survival: one obvious result was longer legs with fewer toes to make for more speedy flight. Some herbivores developed formidable horns, though defence does not seem to have been their primary purpose, and body colouring which could serve either as camouflage or to give warning signals. Fossil records show that even-toed and odd-toed ungulates, the two major groups of herbivorous animals, have evolved separately for at least 60,000,000 years. The evolutionary process has reached its most advanced stage in the antelopes: 'the perfection of ruminant life' according to Sir Julian Huxley.

Black Duiker: Duikers have a distinctive tuft of hair on the crown of their heads

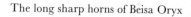

The long sharp horns of Beisa Oryx

Wildebeest are rarely silent

The little Suni

The earliest recognizable ancestors of modern antelopes evolved in northern Africa during the Miocene. These were quite small animals without horns but with little tusks in their upper jaws, like modern musk deer. From these beginnings they gradually spread over a considerable part of the Old World, adapting themselves to a wide variety of habitats as they did so. By the Pliocene there were many different kinds of antelope in Asia and Europe as well as Africa: there were even gazelles in Britain. But, during the climatic upheavals of the Pleistocene, most antelopes left the northern regions while remaining abundant in Africa and plentiful in central and southern Asia. They have not been recorded further east than the island of Celebes.

Antelopes never reached the New World. Other *Bovidae*, such as bison and musk oxen, occur there and deer are widely distributed. But the pronghorn (*Antilocapra americana*) of the western plains, the nearest approach to an antelope among the myriad wild inhabitants of the Americas, is not of the *Bovidae* family. It has branched horns whose outer horny sheath is shed and renewed annually giving it many of the characteristics of a deer. This beautiful and unique animal was almost exterminated in the nineteenth century. But, thanks to careful and intelligent conservation, herds have again built up; pronghorns are now quite numerous in Texas, New Mexico and Montana.

Two members of the *Bovidae* family that can be regarded as borderline antelopes are the nilghai, or blue bull, of India and the smaller Asiatic four-horned antelope. These animals are so unlike other antelopes that it is difficult to think of them as such. Hindus look upon the nilghai, which they will not harm, as a wild relation of their sacred cows. It was described by the Zoological Society of London in 1835: 'In captivity it is gentle, licking the hands of those that offer it bread. There are, however, seasons when it becomes capricious in its temper. When meditating an attack it falls suddenly upon its fore-knees, shuffles onward in that posture until it has advanced to within a few paces of the object of its irritation, and then darts forward with a powerful spring and butts in the most determined manner. Its walk is awkward in consequence of the comparative shortness of its hind legs.'

Systematists are by no means agreed about *Bovidae* taxonomy, but antelopes are generally divided into eight groups most conveniently considered as subfamilies. Each subfamily has its own characteristics and embraces a variable number of genera, species and subspecies. A complete list of species, together with brief descriptive notes, will be found in the appendix. Subspecies. largely a matter of geographical distribution, have been generally ignored in this book. The subfamilies are:

Tragelaphinae: the twist-horned antelopes, typified by the bushbuck and including the nyalas, kudus, and the sitatunga in which the males only carry horns; and the elands and bongo with horns carried by both sexes. These antelopes have a tendency to striped markings on the flank. They have relatively short naked muzzles, no facial or pedal glands but most species have glands in the inguinal region.

Cephalophinae: the duikers. These are small or medium-sized antelopes with robust bodies, rather short legs, a distinctive tuft of hair on the crown of their heads and obvious facial glands. Short straight horns are carried by the males only in some species and by both sexes in others. There are three kinds of duiker: the common bush duiker, several species of forest duiker and the little blue duikers. Duikers are primitive antelopes which have changed little since the days of their ancestor *Eocerus*, a straight-horned animal the size of a sheep.

Reduncinae: the marsh antelopes namely the waterbucks, lechwes, reedbucks, kob, puku, and the vaal rhebok. They are large or medium-sized antelopes whose well ridged horns have a tendency to curve forward at the tip and are carried only by the males. Muzzles are hairless; pedal glands are always present; some species also have facial and inguinal glands.

Hippotraginae: the sabre-horned antelopes comprising the roan and sable antelopes, three species of oryx and the addax. These are large sturdy antelopes with long sharp horns carried by both sexes. They have vividly distinctive facial markings; their skulls are heavy and their muzzles short. Pedal glands are well developed.

Alcelaphinae: the wildebeests and hartebeests. Also included in this subfamily are the so-called bastard hartebeests namely the topi, sassaby, blesbok, bontebok and Hunter's hartebeest. They are relatively large antelopes with high shoulders and backs which slope down to the hindquarters. They are long

Horns of the Greater Kudu: the most magnificent adornment of any horned animal anywhere

A herd of Wildebeest on the move

OPPOSITE: Guenther's Dikdik in the African
bush country

OPPOSITE: The East African grasslands: Impala approach a pool already occupied by flamingoes

Oribi in the long grass

in the skull, have long narrow faces, well developed facial glands and glands above their hoofs. In some species the curved and heavily ridged horns, which are carried by both sexes, rise from a distinct pedicle on the crown.

Neotraginae: the pigmy antelopes including the klipspringer, oribi, grysbok, steinbok, suni, royal and Bates' pigmy antelopes, dikdiks, and the beira. This is rather a miscellaneous collection of small antelopes with short straight horns, usually carried by the males only, and well developed facial glands. All except the dikdiks, which have a tuft of hair on their foreheads, have naked muzzles.

Antilopinae: the gazelles and their relatives. This subfamily includes the Indian blackbuck, the impala, springbok, gerenuk, dibatag and fourteen species of gazelle. These are graceful, slender-limbed antelopes of medium size with shapely horns, carried by both sexes in most of the gazelles but otherwise by the males only. They tend to have markings on the flank and face which is relatively short and narrow. They have pedal glands, and most have pocket-like facial glands.

Caprinae: goat-like antelopes, namely the saiga and the chiru or Tibetan antelope. These palaearctic antelopes are mainly distinguished by enlarged muzzles and inflated nasal passages. This is considered to be an adaptation to the dusty environments in which both these animals live; it is not now thought to have anything to do with the rarefied atmosphere of the high Tibetan plateau, occupied by the chiru. Upright horns are carried only by the males. The saiga, but not the chiru, has well developed scent glands beneath the eyes and on the legs; its yellow-brown coat turns white in winter.

Antelopes are not noisy animals, such sounds as they do make tending to vary with the circumstances and to be peculiar to the species. Wildebeest, however, are rarely silent. They snort, bleat, grunt, moo and blow through their nostrils; and they prance, frisk and whisk their tails so violently that you can hear a herd of wildebeest a long way off. Hartebeest sneeze loudly whenever they toss their heads possibly because of irritation caused by worms in their nostrils. And, in spite of its diminutive size, the little suni has developed a wider range of sounds than most antelopes: a bark when a distant threat is suspected, a sharp whistling snort if the danger is close, and a gurgling goat-like bleat produced by the males

Gerenuk standing on their hind legs

at pairing time. When eland are feeding they low and flick their tails like cattle. Most other twist-horned antelopes bark, particularly when alarmed. The bushbuck's bark is familiar to most people who have spent any length of time in the bush and can easily be mistaken for the sawing grunt of a leopard.

Bushbuck stay alone or in pairs, in forest or thick woodland, and are widely distributed. Eland live in the savanna and run together in herds. The bongo, a magnificent chestnut-red creature sometimes called 'forest eland', is found only in the depths of the forest and is seldom seen. The sitatunga lives in the papyrus swamps, grazing at night on the short grass of the verges. It has long splayed hoofs which enable it to move easily through its bogland home. But, using dogs, it is not difficult to drive sitatunga into the water where poachers hunt them from canoes, causing them to submerge with only their nostrils showing above the surface.

The horns of the greater kudu, three times twisted in a graceful spiral, are probably the most magnificent adornment of any horned animal anywhere. Not uncommon in southern Africa, in East Africa kudu occur only in remote inaccessible and stony country where they are extremely difficult to track. You rarely see a complete hoof-print, and their droppings are small hard pellets easily overlooked; kudu also have remarkably acute senses. I was once looking for these superb antelopes in the Karamoja mountains and knew that they were close from signs of recent feeding. I sat hidden in the undergrowth, and soon four hinds moved into a clearing across a shallow valley. Then I saw a single bull, superbly horned. He was sensitive and suspicious, and he turned almost immediately to disappear with a bark by the way he had come, followed by the hinds.

Duikers are found throughout the greater part of Africa wherever there is forest or thick bush, the common grey duiker being one of the most successful and ubiquitous animals on the continent. When alarmed, duikers dive hastily for cover – the name means 'diver' in Afrikaans – and this habit is probably responsible for the unusual thickening of the frontal region of their skulls. Except for the banded and the yellow-backed species, all forest duikers are very much alike. The yellow-backed duiker, known disparagingly as 'bush-goat' in West

Africa in spite of its striking appearance, is much larger than the others though it invariably walks with its head close to the ground. At times, also, it makes a nest for itself underneath a fallen tree and is one of the very few antelopes to do anything of the kind. The little blue duikers also live in the evergreen forests; they would be extremely difficult to see but for the way in which they flick their tails, exposing the white under-side, as they scuttle into the undergrowth whistling and usually following well used trails.

Many years ago I had a tame reedbuck which was never confined and used to dash round a large garden with the strange rockinghorse motion of its species. Reedbuck emit a loud and high-pitched whistling snort through their nostrils; this animal would whistle away like this whenever it saw a sausage or any other of its species delicacies. Its great friend was an Alsatian dog. They would sit together on the floor in a room full of people, the buck calmly chewing the cud.

None of the other marsh antelopes produces any very obvious sound. Nor are they as closely attached to a marshy habitat as is the sitatunga. But the lechwes are swamp-dwellers. Though seriously reduced in numbers, they are still present in their thousands on the Barotse flood plains and the Kafue flats in Zambia. They splash about in the shallow water as they feed on submerged vegetation surrounded by pelicans, herons, ibises, ducks and geese; at times, too, they lay their graceful horns along their backs and bound through the water with surprising ease. Both kob and waterbuck usually stay fairly close to water. Waterbuck frequently enter lakes or rivers where they show little fear of crocodiles; it is possible, indeed, that their unpleasant musky odour discourages crocodiles from attacking them. Like most antelopes, they swim well and have been known to swim from the mainland to islands several miles out in Lake Victoria. The waterbuck, with its shaggy coat and fine upstanding carriage, reminds one strongly of red deer or wapiti. There are two recognized species, mainly distinguished by the shape of the white patch on their rumps. The common waterbuck occurs in southern Africa and to the east of the great rift valley. And, though the defassa water-buck replaces it further west, the two species are found together in parts of Kenya where they actually interbreed. The western Uganda defassa waterbuck are particularly fine specimens and carry splendid horns. One familiar old male died of old age in the Queen Elizabeth National Park while I was living there. Its perfectly matched horns, now mounted in the safari lodge, came within a fraction of an inch of the world hunting record.

Both the kob and puku, which are closely related are smaller than the waterbuck. In the Kob there is a remarkable variation in colour and coat-markings of individual animals, with the kob in particular showing a marked tendency to albinism – there is also a white-eared race in the Sudan. A large herd in the Murchison Park includes individuals of widely different appearance; some have hides flecked with white, others with darker patches. The paler animals demonstrate almost every intermediate stage between a silvery roan and dull white. Many years ago, too, there was an albino herd near Lake Victoria. But these unique animals were exterminated in a futile and wickedly destructive drive to eliminate tsetse fly which do not feed on kob and rarely even settle on anything white. I have heard of individual waterbuck, bushbuck, topi and duikers with albino characteristics, and a small herd of albino blackbuck has recently been built up in captivity in India.

The sable is generally thought of as the most spectacular of the antelopes. With their necks arched, their heads high and their manes tossing in the breeze, there is a rare distinction about the sable. They seem to know their own superiority and other antelopes give way when a sable approaches a water hole. Should they ignore its presence, a quick sideways shake of the great head soon shows who is the master. Like the sable, the roan antelope is an animal of the woodlands where the colour of its coat provides an excellent camouflage; the black and white facial markings blend perfectly with the shadows and the sunlight.

To most people the word 'antelope' suggests the great herds of game on the African grassland plains; the typical animals of this habitat are the wildebeest and the various hartebeests, almost all of which run together in large herds often in association with other species. High shoulders and long faces give the hartebeests an awkward, stupid appearance which belies acute senses, an exceptionally fast gallop, and great powers of endurance. The wildebeest (or 'gnu' which derives from the

Sable antelope on the Shimba hills in Kenya

Hottentot name for these animals) occurs in enormous numbers on the plains. These antelopes look rather like miniature buffaloes but only the black wildebeest of South Africa can be described as at all pugnacious. With horns that curve viciously forward like meat hooks, black wildebeest drive away strangers that try to join the herd; the females frequently attack their own young.

There are minor differences in shape, and considerable differences in size, between the hoofs of the various antelopes so that you can easily learn to distinguish the species by their tracks. Exceptional developments are evident in certain species, such as the enormously long hoofs of the sitatunga and the somewhat less elongated hoofs of the lechwes. The addax has short and very broad hoofs which allow this oryx-like antelope to move easily in the loose desert sand. The klipspringer's hoofs are cylindrical and feel like hard rubber. With feet together, this compact little animal stands poised on the tips of its hoofs; then it bounds with quite staggering agility across the steep and precarious rocks on which it lives. A tame klipspringer I once kept moved like a skater on a highly polished floor where almost any other hoofed animal would have lain helplessly spread-eagled.

One or other of the pigmy antelopes is found in almost every habitat in Africa. Smallest of them all is the royal antelope of the equatorial rain forest, less than a foot high and the smallest ruminant in the world; it is capable, even so, of clearing over eight feet in a single jump. The suni, another very small antelope, lies up close to the ground like a hare and has deep open facial glands which give out a strong musky odour. The little dikdiks differ from these other miniature antelopes chiefly in the formation of the nose and upper lip which is elongated to form a small prehensile snout useful for stripping leaves and shoots from coarse thorn bushes. In suitable country you often see dikdik out in the open in the early morning. They rush away with frisky leaps and bounds, following well used trails.

The oribi, largest of this subfamily, is an exceptionally delicate animal which always looks sleek and well groomed. Usually seen in pairs, I once counted thirteen oribi together; they seemed to explode from the grass in all directions when I chanced upon them. They are often to be seen bounding through the long grass, whistling loudly and displaying their white tails, or just galloping flat out with their bellies close to the ground. Only the gazelles, with their slender limbs and beautiful far-seeing eyes, can match the oribi for sleek grace. They are perhaps the most typical animals of the drier regions of the Old World. Most gazelles are fawn coloured with a dark band on their flanks bordering their white bellies; the desert gazelles are paler in colour and less obviously marked. In two of the Asian species, the Persian gazelle and the zeren, the males develop noticeably swollen throats during the breeding season. Few other mammals give any comparable outward sign of being in breeding condition.

The long-legged, long-necked gerenuk is an aberrant gazelle with the strange habit of standing on its hind legs to browse thorn bushes which would otherwise be out of reach – an activity made possible by an unusual adaptation of the hip joint. The animal skulks through the scrub, holding its head, which it seems to find too heavy for its neck, below the line of its back. Though well enough known today, the gerenuk was not 'discovered' until 1878. Even so, it is by no means the latest discovery among the antelopes: the mountain nyala was not seen by a European until 1910.

The springbok could properly be described as the southern gazelle but for a different tooth structure and the deep fold of white-haired skin which lies along the centre line of its back. When the animal is excited, this is expanded into an erect crest and the springbok leaps eight or ten feet into the air, several times in quick succession, in an action known as 'pronking'. Stiff-legged, with hoofs bunched tightly together, the animal bounds up and down as if on springs. Like the springbok, but unlike the true gazelles, both the impala and blackbuck are jumpers; they are also capable of incredible turns of speed. In 1890 Sir Samuel Baker wrote of the black-buck in *Wild Beasts and their ways*: 'Away they fly, hardly touching the ground with their swift hoofs but hopping almost vertically in the air and bounding six feet in height at each leap as they follow each other at fifty miles an hour across the level plain.' This might well have been written of the impala, a much more familiar animal today. There is superb elegance in the movements of impala; they seem to flow over the ground, clearing the obstacles in their path with effortless ease.

Long-legged, long-necked Gerenuk

CHAPTER TWO

Distribution, habitat and food

Antelopes of one kind or another live in almost every habitat and every part of Africa. All the Asian antelopes are animals of the deserts, steppes or open plains. Yet fossil remains of many forms, almost identical with modern African forest antelopes, have been found in different parts of Asia; ancestral bushbuck, duikers, and even kudu have appeared in the Indian Pliocene. While such animals as the duikers retreated into the African forests, the forests of Asia were occupied by various deer which, for some reason not known to us, proved the more successful in these surroundings. Nevertheless, gazelles and a few other antelopes remained widely distributed on the central Asian steppes and in suitable country south of the Himalaya. As there have never been deer in Africa south of the Sahara, the African antelopes escaped this competition.

It is impossible nowadays to produce an overall picture of the antelope situation for the whole of Asia. We do not know what animals survive in Manchuria, nor can we assess the present status of the chiru or of the Tibetan gazelle. But, thanks to R.A.Hibbert, we at least have some information from Mongolia, almost the centre of the continent. The Mongolian gazelle is still well distributed on parts of the Gobi steppe where controlled culling is carried out. The black-tailed, goitred gazelle is also present in fair numbers, and the saiga is on the increase.

The saiga is the success story of the antelope world. During the Pleistocene there were saiga in England and throughout eastern Europe and Siberia. Two hundred years ago, they were still plentiful but restricted to the steppes of southern

OPPOSITE (ABOVE): Arabian Gazelle on the desert: singularly harsh conditions

OPPOSITE (BELOW): The Indian Gazelle: Gazelle used to be plentiful on the Indian plains

Russia and central Asia. Chiefly due to the Chinese belief that the horns have medicinal qualities, numbers continued to decline until the early 1900s when only about a thousand saiga remained in small scattered herds in Kazakhstan. Man then acted to save this antelope from what appeared to be inevitable extinction. Hunting was forbidden. The position gradually improved and in 1950 there came a population explosion. Once again saiga were to be seen west of the Volga river. With an estimated population of nearly 3,000,000 the saiga is now the most numerous wild ungulate in the Soviet Union where scientific management has been introduced.

The control of hunting could not alone have achieved this result; the virtual extermination of wolves, the saiga's exceptional fecundity and migratory habits have also been contributory factors. Saiga give birth to their first fawns when just over a year old; and, as twins are common, the population can increase by over fifty per cent each year. With the coming of winter, the saigas move south away from the advancing snow, feeding on shrubs and salt-marsh grasses. They cross the Volga and enter the frozen reedbeds of the Caspian where some perish in the deeper snowdrifts. But eventually they find less severe conditions, and there they stay until spring encourages them to return.

The blackbuck and gazelle used to be plentiful on the grassy plains and *maidans* of a large part of the Indian subcontinent. They survive today in only a few areas such as the rolling Kanha hills in Madhya Pradesh. Here the blackbuck enjoys ideal conditions of good grazing and plentiful shade. But the majority of Asian antelopes, as well as those of some African habitats, live under singularly harsh conditions.

To survive at all in the arid steppes and deserts of the world any animal must achieve a high degree of physiological adaptation. Food is often scarce and of small value in terms of calories. Water shortage is accentuated by low humidity and extreme temperatures. Not only must an animal regulate its body temperature, it must also control loss of water by limiting evaporation through the skin, reducing the volume of urine passed and producing exceptionally dry faeces. We do not know how desert antelopes manage this but they probably function similarly to camels. (Camels can withstand water loss equal to a quarter of their own weight and they can

The Saiga: success story of the antelope world; note also the inflated nasal passages

OPPOSITE: Zebra and Wildebeest graze together below the dome of Kilimanjaro

25

tolerate much greater fluctuations in body temperature than most mammals. They sweat little and their urine is highly concentrated. Again, camels drink large amounts of water whenever they get the chance, though they do not carry a reserve supply in their stomachs as is sometimes suggested; and their humps provide a most efficient system of fat-storage as do the humps of zebu cattle and the tails of African sheep.)

The Arabian oryx, which shares some of the worst deserts in the world with the rhim gazelle, has a shiny coat and fur thick enough to act as insulation against the sun. It is also adept at finding shade in the most unlikely places. It feeds on the sparse desert grasses, herbs and shrubs, using its hoofs to dig out the roots which supply much of the fluid it needs. The rhim gazelle, but not the dorcas which loses weight rapidly if unable to drink, survives in the same conditions. Even so, many antelopes die of starvation in the years of drought when nothing succeeds in growing. Their present scarcity, however, is not due to these conditions but to uncontrolled hunting and human disturbance.

In Africa there is a clear pattern in the distribution of the antelopes and to see this you must look upon the continent as a unit. The heart of Africa is the evergreen tropical rain forest which stretches along the equator from the west coast to the great lakes. Immediately to the north and south of the forest are the wet savanna woodlands where the dry seasons are more marked and trees shed their leaves, though rainfall is still plentiful. These woodlands enclose the forest in a great horseshoe: the Guinea savanna, the Nile basin and the great lakes, and the southern *Brachystegia* woodlands. Further north and south again, as you approach the deserts of the Sahara and the Kalahari, is the dry savanna bushland dominated by acacias, thorn scrub and baobab trees: the Sudanese steppes, the Horn of Africa, the East Africa thornbush and the southern bushveld.

Intruding into the savannas are stretches of rain forest, mostly along riverbanks, and the main highland areas of the continent: these are the mountains of East Africa and Ethiopia, the East African grasslands with their wonderful concentration of wild antelopes, and the South African highveld where few large mammals now survive. Between the dry bushland and the Indian Ocean, a narrow lush coastal strip stretches from Kenya to Zululand. All these vegetation belts gradually merge into each other and there are numerous minor variations to the pattern – for example, the Queen Elizabeth National Park in Uganda is part of the wet savanna but includes forest, thorn scrub and land that can almost be described as desert.

Not many wild animals survive at the extremities of the continent. There are a few gazelles in North Africa: Cuvier's gazelle in the foothills and mountain valleys, dorcas on the plains, and rhim on the sand areas of the open desert. But the bubal hartebeest has been extinct for a hundred years. Antelopes in small numbers still exist at the Cape, chiefly in the hills where there is cover enough for duikers and grysbok, and grass for the vaal rhebok; the latter are primitive animals, and they gallop about the highveld fighting among themselves and attacking the sheep and goats that share their grazing. But little remains of the once abundant wildlife of the lowlands. The blue antelope or blauwbok, a small maneless roan unique to this region, has been extinct since the eighteenth century, and the bontebok almost went the same way.

In the process of evolution animals become adapted to their surroundings. Conditions in Africa repeat themselves as we have seen, so it is only to be expected that the wildlife should do the same. The antelopes of the Guinea savanna are similar to those of the *Brachystegia* woodlands, as are those of the Sudanese steppes and the southern bushveld. The northern gazelles and the beisa oryx balance the springbok and the gemsbok. There are kob in the north and puku in the south, lechwe in the swamps of the Upper Nile and in Zambia but nowhere in between. There are northern and southern hartebeests, wildebeests, elands, and roan antelopes: different species but basically the same animals. Today, of course, these antelopes are largely restricted to reserves and wilderness areas not yet occupied by man.

Very little light filters through the canopy of tall trees in the evergreen tropical forests. Movement is restricted by creepers, shrubs, under-storey trees and fallen trunks. Rain drips down. Moss, ferns, and orchids abound, but there is no grass for grazing animals. Forest duikers are plentiful throughout the forest belt where they feed on leaves, shoots, fruits and berries. Blue duikers, in particular, eat the various fruits

Blue Duiker eat fruits dropped by monkeys

27

Portrait of a young Bushbuck

dropped by monkeys as they scamper overhead. The splendid bongo, most colourful of the antelopes, and the tiny royal antelope share the forests with them. The bushbuck is absent from the depths of the Congo forest but is common where forest breaks into the savanna.

Forest antelopes tend to be both smaller and redder than related species occupying more open habitats. The bongo is a large animal but is much smaller than the eland. Forest bushbuck are quite distinct from the darker bushbuck of the more open woodlands; bushbuck vary considerably according to habitat, those living at high altitudes being the largest and darkest. Most forest duikers are red as are, for example, the red river hog and the forest buffalo. Small size can be explained by diet and the greater ease with which a small animal can move about in the undergrowth. In most of these antelopes, the red coat is accompanied by vertical flank-stripes. The result is that these animals are difficult to see in the shadows and among the trunks of the forest trees, an excellent example of disruptive camouflage colouration.

Conditions comparable to those of the rain forest can be found on some of the higher mountains though the vegetation is quite distinct: forests of bamboo, giant heathers forty feet tall and boggy alpine moorland dominated by gigantic lobelias and groundsels. Many rain forest animals occur, the bushbuck and various duikers being the most widely distributed antelopes. Only the duikers live permanently above 12,000 feet, and I have seen them higher than this in the Ruwenzori mountains. There are mountain reedbuck on the moorland of most of the more open ranges. And eland, which are great wanderers, occasionally visit the heights: they are sometimes seen at nearly 15,000 feet on Kilimanjaro where they feed on the everlasting *Helichrysum*.

Bongo live on several of the Kenya mountains: notably Mount Kenya, the Aberdare range and the Mau. They browse young bamboo shoots and mountain lobelias and they eat stinging nettles, bark, rotting wood, roots and bulbs. Bongo usually forage alone and at night but congregate in quite large parties during the day when they normally lie up in the thickest fastnesses of the bamboo forest. They are exceptionally wary, their enormous ears picking up the slightest sound; they themselves move quite silently, crawling under low branches instead of jumping over them. Bongo travel extensively to visit favourite salt-licks which are an important source of minerals to many antelopes. Where there are no salt-licks forest duikers occasionally feed on carrion and kill small birds.

The Ethiopian highlands form the largest single mountain bloc in Africa. Cut by deep gorges and bounded by the thorn scrub of the Horn of Africa, the high plateau of Ethiopia rises

Bongo usually forage alone

Topi herd in the red oat grass

Jackson's Hartebeest standing sentinel on an ant-hill by the Albert Nile

up in a series of floral zones related to altitude; these culminate in evergreen forest and alpine vegetation. Most of the forest has been destroyed and, with it, a great deal of the wildlife. There are kudu, bushbuck, waterbuck and duikers in the foothills and oryx in some of the valleys. But wild animals survive in significant numbers in only a few parts of the highlands. One of these is the Mendebos mountains, south of Addis Ababa, the entire range of the mountain nyala. Small herds of these superb antelopes, whose total population is probably less than 4,000, wander among the giant heathers and *Hypericum* trees of the moorland at 10,000 to 13,000 feet. They eat grass, herbs, moss and clover as well as various leaves; and they descend to the cedar belt when they want a change of diet. Little is known about these rare and secretive animals whose wild mountain habitat is shared by the dark Ethiopian bushbuck, the klipspringer and the Simien fox. A national park is being planned for their protection.

The lowland or Zululand nyala is the most important surviving antelope of the coastal strip where wild animals once swarmed: it can be seen in several reserves including the Lengwe Reserve in Malawi. Like its namesake, this nyala both grazes and browses. But its distribution is so limited as to suggest some special food requirement, possibly the fallen fruits and pods of a riverain mahogany with which this antelope is usually associated. The little suni is also found throughout the bushland of the coastal strip. It feeds on fruits and berries but also shows a marked addiction to a single food plant: the carrot-like roots of a local umbellifer. An isolated herd of sable antelope live on the Shimba hills a few miles from the Kenya port of Mombasa.

The Guinea savanna stretches across the continent from Senegal to the valley of the Nile and the great lakes. The savanna belt is unbroken, but the lake region is more mountainous and more varied. This fertile part of Africa is heavily populated by man except where tsetse fly has made it uninhabitable. Such areas support a greater total weight of wild animal life to the square mile (usually described as 'biomass') than anywhere else on earth: elephants, hippopotamuses and buffaloes as well as antelopes. There are important reserves, notably the Queen Elizabeth and Murchison Falls National Parks, in Uganda, and the Albert and Garamba National Parks in the Congo and the Sudan's great Southern National Park.

Much of the country is orchard bush: *Isoberlinia*, *Terminalia*, and butternut trees in the tall *Hyparrhenia* grasslands. True 'elephant grass', avoided by antelopes, only occurs where the soil is particularly rich. There are short grass areas with desert dates, figs, borassus palms and tamarinds; and rolling plains of red oat grass, studded with acacias, which is much sought after by grazing antelopes. They nibble the fresh green shoots after the annual burn; at the end of the rains they can be seen in the mature grass which then looks like ripening corn.

The most important antelopes of the wet savanna are the hartebeests and the topi – both found throughout the grasslands of Africa – the defassa waterbuck, the kob and the bohor reedbuck. The graceful little oribi is widely distributed. Bush duikers occur wherever there are thickets, varying their diet with the seasons but picking much of it from the ground, including fallen fruits and fungi. All antelopes have slightly different food requirements and this determines the detail of their distribution within the major habitats. The waterbuck prefers well wooded savanna and alluvial plains, and stays remarkably faithful to one locality. Both kob and reedbuck eat the red oat grass and avoid the coarser, less palatable grasses eaten by hartebeest. Hartebeest live in drier stretches of the savanna where the grazing herds are guarded by sentinels which watch for danger, usually from flat-topped anthills. During the hottest hours of the day, hartebeest move to the shade of nearby trees. Roan antelope, more numerous in the southern savanna, prefer wooded valleys through which they wander in single file.

Lord Derby's giant eland is found from Senegal to the Uganda border, but there are wide gaps in its distribution and it is becoming increasingly rare. This magnificent animal lives in thick bush, feeding on the leaves and pods of the *Isoberlinia* trees, breaking off the branches with its horns. It eats bulbs, aloes, and a yellow-flowered gardenia; it will also nibble grass. Giant eland are wary and travel long distances at a fast walk, browsing as they go. This makes them remarkably difficult to find even when you know quite well that you are close to a herd that you have been following for days.

The great swamps of the Nile and the smaller swamps of Uganda form a distinct habitat within the savanna. Sitatunga,

Sitatunga: once plentiful

The right habitat for Klipspringer

once plentiful, have been greatly reduced by poaching. In spite of a much more restricted distribution, chiefly the swamps of the Bahr-el-ghazal and the Sobat, Nile lechwe remain reasonably numerous thanks to the traditional protection accorded them by members of the Shilluk tribe. Nile lechwe feed on swamp and aquatic vegetation, such as water lilies, but sometimes join the white-eared kob to graze on the riverside flats. These swamp-dwelling antelopes are seldom bothered by crocodiles which feed mainly upon fish.

The southern *Brachystegia* woodlands, or *Miombo*, balances the Guinea savanna. It is an immense wilderness area embracing the southern Congo, Angola, Zambia, Mozambique, and a considerable part of Tanzania. Although there is no exact parallel to the basin of the Nile, the great valleys and fertile flood plains of the Zambesi and its tributaries (particularly the Kafue and Luangwa rivers) provide comparable conditions and support great concentrations of game. Puku, waterbuck and buffaloes are plentiful. Lechwe, nowadays, are found only on the flood plains and in a few swamps such as the Bangweulu where the black lechwe lives. Though lechwe sometimes wade up to their bellies to feed on aquatic weeds, they prefer to graze where shallow water just covers the grassy plains. They ruminate on dry land, usually on ant-hills or sandy spits.

Most of this savanna belt consists of tall grass and scattered trees growing on poor sandy soils where human population is generally sparse. Rocky inselbergs provide the right habitat for klipspringer which eat grasses as well as succulent plants and which drink irregularly, usually at night. Broad-leaved *Mopane* trees occur in extensive patches of thicker woodland such as the Luangwa valley, one of the richest game areas in southern Africa, and the Wankie National Park.

Lichtenstein's hartebeest, probably the most widely distributed of Zambia's larger antelopes, replaces the northern hartebeests. The puku takes the place of the kob, and the common reedbuck that of the bohor. There are roan antelope, oribi, and duikers in both savannas. The giant eland is matched by the sable antelope, more numerous and even more splendid in its natural home among the *Mopane* trees. Greater kudu and eland are plentiful, particularly in the Wankie, but are typical animals of the drier bushveld further south. The impala, the steinbok, and the grysbok are widely distributed.

Short grass steppe separates the Guinea savanna from the Sahara. Acacias, desert dates and doum palms grow along the water courses. Elsewhere trees are small except for the baobab. Rainfall is uncertain, the animals are unevenly distributed and migratory. The topi is the most widely distributed antelope. Where the steppe merges into the desert you find oryx, scimitar-horned in the west and beisa oryx further east. These migrate from one grazing area to another, congregating in large herds before they do so. Addax and dama gazelles, which range further south than oryx, leave the deserts occasionally. Soemmering's and Heuglin's gazelles are found on the eastern part of the steppe; the korin occurs in West Africa; there are kudu in the hills. The higher rainfall and lush grasses of Lake Chad and the Futa Jallon highlands bring marsh antelopes to the steppe.

Many of the antelopes from this part of Africa occur in Dinder National Park in the eastern Sudan. And in the Ileme Triangle, where the steppe abuts against the Ethiopian highlands, is one of the continent's greatest remaining concentrations of wildlife. This huge area, waterless thornbush in dry weather and a quagmire in the rains, stretches southwards to Lake Rudolph and northern Kenya. When the rivers rise in May, great columns of kob, topi, eland and gazelles move south in enormous numbers. Roan antelope, waterbuck, zebra, and giraffes go with them; but the lesser kudu, which feeds largely on bowstring hemp, rarely leaves the *Commiphora* bush and does not migrate.

The thornbush and arid scrub of the Horn of Africa, a continuation of the steppe, curls around the Ethiopian highlands. Troops of oryx wind their way through the thinly scattered bush. Soemmering's and Pelzeln's gazelles, now rare, live in the northern part of this land. Speke's gazelle stays on the Somali plateau; the males, when excited, develop strangely inflated nostrils. Giraffes, gerenuk, the little beira, and several species of dikdik browse on acacias, each animal feeding at a different height; dikdiks also eat succulents and desert dates. The dibatag feeds on *Commiphora*, a common shrub little eaten by other antelopes. Many animals eat the pulpy fruits of the baobab. Greater and lesser kudus occur, the former on the hills, the latter on the plains. The greater kudu ranges from

Gemsbok in the Kalahari

Never again will anyone witness the fabulous migration of the Springbok

Lake Chad to southern Africa but distribution is very broken, probably because this antelope is so susceptible to rinderpest. Many of the thorn scrub antelopes can be seen in the new Awash National Park in Ethiopia.

The steppe gradually merges into the sands and stony wastes of the Sahara where, to exist at all, animals must compete with conditions similar to Arabia. The addax, the scimitar-horned oryx, and certain gazelles thrive in the open desert. The dame gazelle prefers the desert fringes. The addax still survives in Darfur and the Hoggar mountains but has been virtually exterminated elsewhere. Though usually seen alone or in pairs, larger numbers occasionally congregate.

South of the *Brachystegia* woodlands, the bushveld stretches across Africa from Swaziland to the Atlantic. Though conditions are less severe, both flora and fauna have much in common with the East African thornbush. The bushveld includes some of the best game areas of the continent: Kruger National Park, the Okovango swamps and the Makarikari pans. Impala, either grazing or browsing as opportunity offers, are abundant in the Kruger which is the true home of the superb greater kudu. There are roan antelope, sable, wildebeest, and hartebeest. The sassaby, the southern topi and one of the speediest of antelopes, is plentiful. There are steinbok, oribi, and duikers but no gazelles and no dikdiks. The klipspringer lives on kopjes and rocky hills.

The sandy plains of northern Botswana support spectacular herds of antelopes which concentrate around Okovango and Makarikari in astonishing numbers and even more astonishing variety. Bushveld and woodland animals are brought together by the only water within miles. And, as happens near Lake Chad, the swamps bring water-loving species into contact with those of a drier habitat. Nomadic desert animals, such as the gemsbok and the springbok, come to the swamps when the drought is severe. Roan, sable, hartebeest, kudu and zebra occur. Wildebeest are present in their thousands. You see eland at their best on the bushveld where they run in small herds.

Tempered by altitude and moisture-laden winds from the Atlantic, the southern deserts, Kalahari and Karoo, are much less severe than the Sahara. But water sinks into the red sands, and there is little vegetation other than desert shrubs and grasses. Bushveld animals visit the deserts, particularly the

Grant's Gazelle on the East African grassland

Cattle bunch together and often cause damage by trampling

red hartebeest which is nomadic and inhabits drier country than its northern relatives. But the typical desert antelopes of the region are the springbok and the gemsbok which augment their diet with bulbs and wild tsama melons.

There used to be millions of springbok on the Karoo and elsewhere in South Africa. Today they are numerous only in the Kalahari-Gemsbok National Park and a few other areas such as the Etosha pans in northern Amboland. Never again will anyone witness the fabulous migration of the springbok, the unexplained *trekbokke* when millions of these animals were on the move. They surged across the country from the deserts to the Cape, plodding slowly on, browsing and nibbling and digging out bulbs with their hoofs, but never drinking and never stopping. They were packed so densely that they trampled underfoot, or just swept along, anything in their way, including such large antelopes as eland and wildebeest. Thousands of springbok were killed or drowned as they surged across great watercourses like the Orange river. After some days the trek would melt away. The springbok never returned. This extraordinary mass migration was periodic, not seasonal. No one knows what made the springbok move.

The East African grasslands, dominated by red oat and other sweet grasses, and generally well studded with tall acacia trees, support the most spectacular concentration of wild mammals left anywhere on earth. There is a higher biomass in the Nile basin but the animals there are fewer in number and heavier in weight. On the Serengeti plains, the heart of the grassland, there are twenty-eight species of antelope as well as such other mammals as giraffes, rhinoceroses, lions, and leopards. The concentration of large antelopes averages some fifty individuals to the square kilometre. There is considerable seasonal variation, but a recent estimate of the total antelope populations has been 600,000 Thomson's and 40,000 Grant's gazelles, up to 450,000 wildebeest, 20,000 topi as well as large numbers of eland, roan antelope, impala, hartebeest, water buck and such smaller animals as duikers, oribi, and steinbok. There are also 170,000 zebra. These grasslands are classified as highlands, ecologically between the wet and the dry savanna. Soils are shallow and thornbush encroaches rapidly when the land is heavily grazed by domestic stock.

Cattle and wild ungulates do not graze in the same way.

Cattle bunch together and often cause considerable damage by trampling. They only eat sweet grasses, leaving untouched those of nutritionally poor quality which then gradually replace more palatable species. And, if only because of the natural indolence of herdsmen, cattle stay where they are until there is nothing left for them to eat. Antelopes always move on. They also feed and travel well spaced out except when fear causes a stampede. They have more efficient digestive systems than cattle and make more economical use of the grassland.

The grasslands evolved in association with the wild ungulates. The different species eat grass at different stages of growth so that grazing is complementary, not competitive. And zebra, with their upper incisor teeth, are able to eat coarser grasses than either cattle or antelopes. Where the wild ungulate population is high, there tends to be a regular grazing sequence. The zebra usually graze first, then wildebeest, hartebeest, and gazelles in that order, so the land is not subjected to the same pressure as when grazed by cattle. Most

Zebra and Wildebeest mass together before the Serengeti migration

grazing antelopes eat legumes, sedges, and clovers as well as grass; this enables them to survive in reasonable health during dry weather when the protein content of most grasses is low. Topi eat older grasses in low-lying swampy areas. Eland, impala and gazelles both browse and graze; they also vary their diets seasonally. Thomson's gazelle are primarily grazers, but about ten per cent of their diet consists of fruits, seeds and pods of high nutritional value. Grant's gazelle adapt easily to change of diet, otherwise they could not thrive equally well in the arid thornbush as they do on the rich pasture of the northern Serengeti.

Migration is another natural device for making the best use of grassland. The famous migration of the Serengeti goes on throughout the year and involves perhaps half a million animals, mainly wildebeest but also zebra and Thomson's gazelle, though the gazelle do not travel as far as the others. In May, or early June, most of the wildebeest leave the short grass plains and gradually disperse to their dry weather refuge areas, 150 miles away in the northern and western areas of the National Park where there is permanent water and plentiful shade. They travel in loose herds followed by the zebra and Thomson's gazelle.

With the second rainy season in November, the herds mass together for their return journey to the short grass plains where the wildebeest normally drop their calves shortly after arrival. If the rains are late, however, the whole operation may be delayed, and the wildebeest may be forced to calve while still travelling. During this phase of the migration, the wildebeest move in long regular columns and follow behind the gazelle and the zebra. The gazelle lead the way back, possibly because they are more sensitive to the wind and temperature changes that indicate distant rain. But no one really knows what triggers off these spectacular migrations, nor can they be timed exactly. It may be the urge of the female wildebeest to seek their habitual breeding places; it could even be influenced by their need to escape from the tiresome biting flies which worry them constantly in the wooded refuge areas but which are absent from the open plains. Like all seasonal animal movements, however, the ultimate cause must be food; the wildebeest leave the plains when food is short and return to calve when the young grass is fresh and green.

Serengeti migration: Wildebeest move in long regular columns

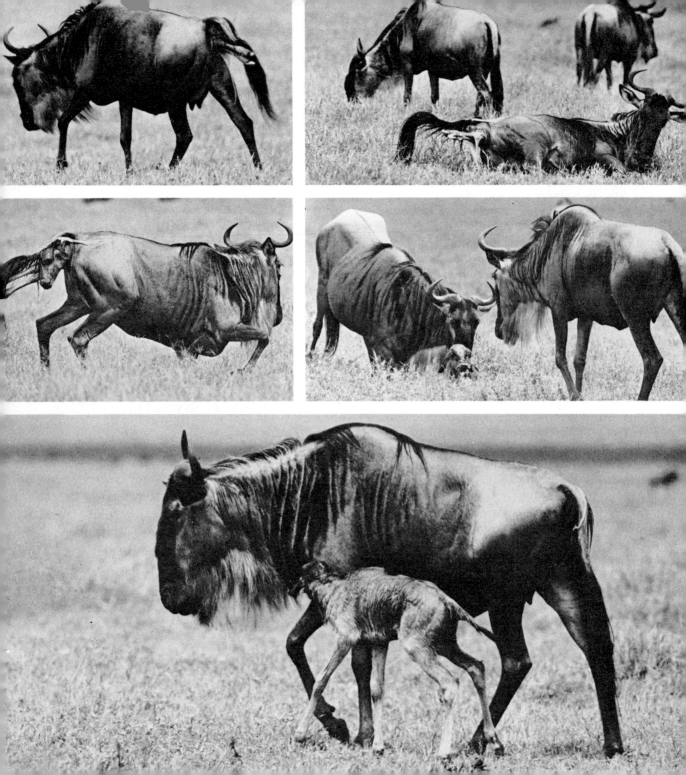

CHAPTER THREE

Herds and individuals

The antelope breeding cycle follows the normal mammalian pattern: oestrus, mating and fertilization, a period of gestation, birth, lactation, and another oestrus. With most of the larger species there is one cycle each year; calves are born at the beginning of the rains when the country is green with the tender shoots of new young grass, and feeding conditions are good. Thus where there is a definite winter, or only one rainy season, there tends to be one breeding season. But there are two wet and two dry seasons on the equator and this means that conditions suitable for calving occur at least twice. In some areas where feeding opportunities change little, and in certain species, calves may be dropped at any time: this is the situation with most forest antelopes and the smaller species generally.

The age at which breeding starts, the period of gestation and the longevity vary considerably, with the larger antelopes tending to breed later and more slowly than the smaller, and to live longer. The eland starts breeding at about three years, the hartebeest at two and the steinbok at nine months – females of the latter come into season for four days at a time every three months. In the common duiker the gestation period averages about four months. With most small antelopes it is between five and seven months: five months has been recorded for Thomson's gazelle; five and a half for the springbok; six and a half for the oribi; seven months for lechwe, reedbuck, and impala; seven and a half to eight months for the topi; eight months for the waterbuck; eight or occasionally nine months for hartebeest, eland, and the sable

Young Guenther's Dikdik

OPPOSITE: The birth of a Wildebeest

39

antelope. The longest recorded gestation period seems to have been three hundred days for a captive beisa oryx.

If you are lucky enough to be in the right place at the right time you may see grazing antelopes calving in the open. But the smaller forest antelopes drop their young in isolation in dense thickets. The birth of such a familiar animal as the impala, which spends an appreciable amount of time in thick woodland, does not seem to have been observed in the wild.

In all antelopes the actual process of parturition is extraordinarily quick. Some of the females remain standing, others lie down. Many young antelopes are on their feet within two minutes of birth; others may take forty or fifty minutes. I was once watching a herd of topi galloping across the grassland when a single female stopped and dropped her fawn. She remained standing throughout, the herd waiting while she licked her baby clean and nuzzled it until it stood up. A warden in Queen Elizabeth Park timed the process: the young topi was on its feet and following the herd within fifteen minutes. Other topi soon began to drop their own calves while the rest of the herd provided a protective screen. This is a necessary precaution, adopted by several species, as hyenas are particularly active at such times; fortunately, however, these unwelcome visitors can usually be driven away.

A female hartebeest has been observed leaving the herd accompanied by another younger female. She moved to high ground but continued to graze, stopping occasionally to lie down and roll, a sign of labour and perhaps of a difficult birth. She lay on the ground, and the calf began to appear head and forefeet first. When the calf was half ejected, the mother stood up allowing it to slip away from her. Then she stripped away the membrane, bit through the umbilical cord and ate the afterbirth, thereby destroying evidence which might otherwise lead a passing predator to her newborn calf. A few minutes later the mother brought the calf to its feet. It then began to suckle and was soon ready to follow the herd. The whole process had taken forty-five minutes. A young wildebeest has been seen to run with the herd within five minutes of its first attempt to stand. Steinbok show signs of labour for several hours though the actual birth, which usually takes place on a patch of bare ground surrounded by long grass,

Grant's Gazelle: most antelope calves wag their tails while suckling

the mother lying down all the time is over within thirty minutes. Most antelope births occur singly. But twins appear with some frequency and triplets have been recorded. The different species show considerable differences in fecundity.

In some species the young fawns move off with the grazing herd as soon as they can walk, though it is common practice for females with very young calves to form nursery herds at this time; topi do so. Thomson's gazelle females tend to form small groups with their young and to stay in the same locality for three or four days. They remain apart from the main herd until lactation is nearly complete and the fawn ready to fend for itself. Most antelopes lactate for three or four months though the young of many species begin to experiment with solid food when about a month old.

Bushbuck and duikers hide their young and leave them in seclusion. Roan antelope do likewise but the young sable immediately runs with the herd. Steinbok keep their fawns hidden safely away in holes underground. Individual female waterbuck leave the herd and stay near their calves which are usually hidden for two or three weeks. Beisa oryx often hide their young alongside sandy stream beds where you sometimes find a crèche of youngsters frolicking together. Young impala are left in thick cover for the first few days though one or two adults always stay on guard. Even when fully capable of keeping pace with their elders, the young of many species tend to hide and not flee from danger.

Most infant antelopes are almost silent though young oribi, reedbuck, and some others bleat faintly before beginning to suckle. But the main method of communication between the infant antelope and its mother is a vigorous prod at the udder. Most antelope calves wag their tails vigorously while suckling. The mother frequently bends her head and sniffs to make sure that she is feeding the right calf. Not only does it carry its own individual smell, it acquires her scent from the greasy skin of her udder.

The age of antelopes can best be determined by studies of their teeth. The milk teeth (incisors and pre-molars) of a young waterbuck begin to erupt within a week of birth and are replaced in the third year. The first permanent molar appears at one year, but full adult dentition is not developed for four years. Thereafter the molars gradually wear down. Smaller

Grant's Gazelle fighting: almost completely
ritualized

antelopes have all their teeth when two or two-and-a-half
years old.

Body size increases rapidly in early life but slows down
sooner in females than in males. Thomson's gazelle are fully
grown at about one year. The larger species take longer.
There is little reliable information about longevity: nine or
ten years seems to be the normal life-span of most small
antelopes, while eighteen or possibly even twenty is probably
the maximum for the largest. Clive Spinage calculates that in
the wild the average life-span of a male waterbuck is eleven
years and of a female thirteen but that, in exceptional circumstances, one might live to be eighteen. A male waterbuck in
a New York zoo has lived to be sixteen-and-a-half.

Horn growth is not a reliable guide to age except when the
animal is very young. The horns of most antelopes first appear
at three or four months and become obvious, in the normal
conditions of field observation, at about six months. Growth
thereafter depends largely upon the size of the antelope. In
the waterbuck, the full adult shape is apparent at two years,
and growth continues until the fifth or sixth year when the
horns are at their most splendid. Later on they may get worn
down. Horns of Thomson's gazelle reach their greatest length
in the third year, shortly after full dentition is achieved. At
one year, the beautiful lyrate horns of the Uganda kob are
just simple spikes. In the second year they hook forward and

look something like the horns of an adult reedbuck. The final shape becomes apparent in the third year.

The earliest ancestral antelopes were hornless. Then came animals with short sharp spikes like modern duikers. Subsequent evolution produced the diverse, curved and twisted horns which now adorn so many antelopes. The diversity of shape is striking, as is the uneven distribution of horns between the sexes. Neither of these facts is easy to explain; though it seems that horns must have different primary functions in different species. In general, however, it is probably safe to say that their social significance within the species is more important than their function as weapons of offence or defence against predators.

Fighting between males of the same species, usually for territory or females, is a common feature of antelope society. But the fighting is almost completely ritualized: more often than not differences are settled by threats and intimidating gestures without a blow being struck. In more serious contests the rivals may butt each other. If horns are brought into active play at all, however, they are usually locked together in such a way that the result is a wrestling match and no actual damage occurs. Horns also serve as organs of display, as symbols of rank within the herd, and probably as identifying marks by means of which individuals are able to recognize each other.

Horns which can be described as really effective weapons are present only in certain antelopes: sable, roan and oryx are outstanding examples of this. These antelopes readily stand or kneel at bay when attacked, and even lions have succumbed to the wicked thrust of their horns. Theirs is the assured aggressive temperament often associated with powerful armament as well as with strongly contrasting facial marking. But when two males of the same species come into conflict, their actions are tempered by strict ritual and they rarely hurt each other. Eland are placid animals, but their horns can also be extremely useful weapons of defence in an emergency. In all these species the females bear horns which are just as effective as the male's. Some strike sideways; others, like the oryx, give an upthrust from below or strike downwards from above.

Some antelopes have horns which are so small and slender

Hornless female Waterbuck

43

that they are obviously useless as weapons of defence against the larger beasts of prey; but they are sharp and may well be effective against small predators. These are mostly small antelopes in which the distribution of horns between the sexes seems most irregular. In several species that live in large herds in which the sexes are roughly equal, for example the hartebeests, both male and female carry horns. Where the males alone have horns, there is a tendency to form smaller herds, usually of one male accompanied by several females. For instance, oribi and reedbuck live in pairs or small groups, and waterbuck herds are small compared with wildebeest or topi. And the great herds of kob and impala are actually subdivided into a number of quite small groups. Some of the gazelles, particularly Thomson's, seem to contradict this pattern. There is a comparable breakdown in the herds, yet both sexes carry horns; those of the female, however, are but weak replicas of the male's.

Certain antelopes bear horns which obviously serve more readily as symbols than as weapons. Others again seem perfectly designed for interlocking and holding in intraspecific ritual wrestling matches. This is probably the most vital single function of horns in the antelope world.

On the banks of the Albert Nile in the Murchison Falls Park there are always herds of hartebeest and kob as well as a few oribi, waterbuck, and usually reedbuck. You see pairs of kob standing face to face, horns more or less parallel. The contestants then try to touch each other by quick movements of the horns which are now lower and pointing forward. They hold this position, waiting to parry the blow which each animal expects. If one kob turns his head the other does the same, as if the two animals were shadow-fighting before a mirror. Their heads get lower and lower and their forelegs further apart. They dart forward and foreheads clash briefly together. Eventually one of the animals submits, turns and runs away. It all suggests a ritual contest, or a game played under strict rules, rather than an actual fight. On another part of the plain a pair of hartebeest are behaving similarly. Rules are not identical, and the fight ends when one male throws his neck across the other as a preliminary to chasing him away. As you watch, two male waterbuck gallop along the river bank: another loser is being seen off.

Wherever there are antelopes in large numbers such scenes are being played out. Two male Thomson's gazelle come into conflict on the Serengeti. Horns are inclined forward, and the two animals move backwards and forwards without actually touching, though a ritualized fight may develop. A pair of impala threaten and circle one another. These happen to be aggressive individuals and a fight develops: they twist and push and butt, and their horns are locked together, but serious injuries rarely result. Wildebeest fight differently again, often going down on their knees, but actual contests develop only where two individuals are equally matched. Otherwise a show of superior horns or a shake of the head is almost always sufficient to subdue a potential rival. Nevertheless, antelopes do not neglect to keep their horns sharp; several species rub them on trees or ant-hills, presumably for this purpose.

We know little about the way in which animals recognize each other as individuals except that they can do so. Horns are almost certainly involved as there are slight differences in the size and shape of the horns of every individual antelope. Facial markings, stripes and bands on the coat probably come into it as, again, every individual has slightly different marks: it is widely believed, for example, that the vertical black streaks on the rumps of impala act as recognition marks. Tail-wagging and voice may also play some part. But smell is undoubtedly the most important means of communication between individual antelopes. In spite of their keen sight and hearing, they depend upon the scent exuded by their various glands for final recognition of their young and their mates. They also leave scent as a signal in places where they wish to discourage rivals or expect to meet others of their own kind.

Many antelopes are notably regular in their habits. Bushbuck frequent the same glades at the same time each evening. Duikers ruminate in the same thickets and hartebeest return to the same trees for their midday rest. Individual antelopes visit the same ant-hills to rub off ticks or to use as observation posts. Such places are often marked by scent. You usually find oribi in the same part of the grassland; they are among the last to leave when the bush fires rage and the first to return to the fire-blackened ground afterwards. They also have the habit, shared by duikers, dikdiks and some other species, of constantly returning to the same place to defecate – a charac-

Bush Duiker: recognition of young by licking and sniffing at scent glands

Oribi defecating at a fixed point

Oribi leaving scent mark on the stem of a plant

teristic habit that means that in captivity these animals are extremely easy to house-train. Defecation at a fixed point is usually, but not always, a means of demarcating territory. Several duikers will often share a single defecating point. And, near salt-licks and water holes, which are rarely included in individual territories, you sometimes find patches of bare ground used for defecation by several species, hyenas as well as antelopes. A dikdik will sometimes place its own deposit on top of elephant or rhino droppings. This has nothing to do with territory.

The graceful little oribi is very familiar in the Murchison Falls Park. You see a single male step daintily from the long grass, stamp his forefeet impatiently and then turn his head in a series of jerky movements. A female joins him; he watches with interest as she urinates and defecates. He approaches and taps the ground with his foot. Then he turns towards the female and sniffs her quarters, drawing back his lips to bare his teeth and flaring his nostrils the better to test her scent and readiness for mating: this action is known to German ethologists as *flehmen*. After this little ceremony the two animals rush off together but are soon back on the home ground.

Oribi have well developed interdigital glands. The male stamps his forefeet to impregnate the ground and the droppings of the female with his own scent. He may also deposit scent on the female's body. The gland in front of the eyes is also highly developed. When the oribi jerks his head, he is scattering scent to place a signal on some nearby shrub. The waxy secretion from this gland is also placed directly on suitable objects. You may see an oribi work the opening of the gland round a reed or a twig as he leaves his mark upon it. Heini Hediger was the first to interpret this kind of scent-marking which he had observed in 1948. Some years before this date I had a tame oribi. It followed my wife around the garden and used to mark the stems when she was cutting flowers. At first we thought it would poke its own eyes out. Then we decided that it was just cleaning the glandular cleft on its face and obviously would not hurt itself. It was many years before we understood what it really had been doing. Most antelopes deposit scent signals though the exact detail of their behaviour differs. You commonly see them sniffing at bushes and dung-heaps. Moreover, scent left on the ground by antelopes with pedal glands almost certainly serves to direct stragglers back to the herd.

The main antelope preoccupations are feeding, resting, escape from enemies, and reproduction. This gives a rhythm to the lives of most antelopes which is broken only during migration and at the height of the breeding season when the males direct all their energies towards the opposite sex and may even stop eating. A typical day in the life of Thomson's gazelle has been described by Alan Brooks. It starts at dawn with the herd on high ground in the open. The animals are well dispersed and feeding; a few are courting; others are fighting in their stereotyped way while the youngsters play. Small parties leave the grazing grounds and walk to the river to drink. With increasing heat, the gazelle become less active. They rest and sleep and chew the cud, idling away the hours. They sit with their backs to the wind, their heads up and their legs either stretched forward or tucked beneath their bellies – ruminants rarely lie on their sides as this position interferes with the smooth working of their complicated digestive systems. By mid-afternoon they begin to become more active; feeding and courting start again. Almost all the animals feed during the last two hours of daylight though some may drink at this time. These activities continue throughout the night except for one or two periods of rest. But this is also the time when enemies are most active.

The need for vigilance never stops. Even when asleep or ruminating, an antelope's senses remain alert to the stimulus of danger and it rarely happens that all the individuals in a herd are asleep at the same time. Some of the less wary species tend to associate with hartebeest, to take advantage of their sentinels, or with giraffes which have an enormous range of vision. Birds also help. Go-away-birds warn antelopes of danger by cackling from branches overhead. Oxpeckers, which perch and search for ticks on the bodies of many species, rise up in alarm from dangers unperceived by their hosts. These are not the only birds which associate with antelopes. Cattle egrets and bee-eaters, particularly, feed on insects disturbed by the grazing herds. At times, also, birds worry antelopes to make them move and thereby disturb more insects. Some antelopes resent this and there are records of pigeons, francolins, and even bustards being killed by

Thomson's Gazelle: even when ruminating an antelope's senses are alert

47

infuriated antelopes chopping at them with their forefeet.

Speed in escape is essential to defence from real dangers. The Indian blackbuck and the Mongolian gazelle have both been credited with sixty miles per hour though the authenticity of this is questionable: forty-five or fifty miles per hour is probably the maximum attainable. Most antelopes walk, trot, gallop and jump with actions characteristic of the species. Impala are the champion jumpers: over thirty feet horizontal and eight feet vertical have been recorded. Even eland jump, as I learned when a tame eland of mine cleared a four-foot fence to get into an experimental cotton plot where it ate a year's research in a single night.

Although there is a surprising diversity in the social behaviour of the different antelopes, the pattern is always determined by the needs of reproduction and survival. Several of the smaller species live alone, pairs coming together only for mating: the suni, most of the duikers, and the grysbok, for example. Dikdik and steinbok are believed to pair for life, and you nearly always see a male and a female together. Oribi and reedbuck may well do so, too: it is, in fact, normal to come upon a mated pair of reedbuck ruminating together in longish grass.

Although usually seen in pairs, sometimes you find quite

Thomson's Gazelle drinking

Female Waterbuck greets a Hammerkop in the
water

large gatherings of reedbuck, and Desmond Vesey-Fitzgerald once came upon an amazing concourse of more than 200 of these animals. A hundred young seemed to be taking part in a wild version of 'follow my leader' while the mature animals stood by. The young reedbuck bounded round in a great circle, their tails erect and their legs straight. Males were following females as they commonly do in courtship chasing. But there was no mating, nor even attempts at mounting; the whole performance was quite silent.

Other antelopes, notably hartebeest and impala, are occasionally observed behaving in a somewhat similar way. Thirty hartebeest, in pairs like circus horses, galloped round and round a large bush while others stood motionless waiting their turn to join in. The impala display, which is quite often observed, is even more impressive, but that is only to be expected of these most distinguished antelopes. A warden in Kagera National Park has described a scene where thirty males left a mixed herd of impala which were browsing in the usual way. Suddenly they started dashing round in circles one behind the other, bellowing 'ro-ro-ro' as loud as they could. Their tails were held high and waving in the air, and their muzzles were pointing upwards. They seemed to be enjoying themselves enormously, but the females paid not the slightest attention and continued to browse. Sometimes you see dikdik circling in pairs, grunting as they run, but this has more obvious sexual significance.

I cannot attempt to explain these complicated ceremonies. They are somewhat reminiscent of roe deer 'rings' where the buck and the doe chase round and round, mating frequently and returning season after season to the same 'rings', which are also used as playgrounds by young animals. But, unlike the antelope ceremonies, these are specifically concerned with breeding. The probable explanation is that it is a ritualized form of play as there is such a marked ritual or ceremonial element in so much antelope behaviour. You often see young antelopes at play while their elders are feeding. They joust, butt, frisk, chase, and jump, learning the actions which will later help them in the struggle for survival. Young impala leave the herd, face each other, turn and twist their heads, and go through the motions of butting. Then they frisk about together for a while and return to the fold.

The social life of herd antelopes, only a few of which have yet been studied in detail, seems to be controlled by three main influences: the territorial instinct, the principle of the harem, and the demands of social status. The result is that their behaviour and attitudes towards other individuals in the same herd have become formal and stereotyped; antelopes act as though governed by well established 'rules'. They do not fight to maim or kill but to establish sexual or social status. Behaviour has become most completely ritualized in the territorial and harem herds. Where status alone is involved, it seems that this can often be established simply by a show of superior strength. The exact constitution of an eland herd is not certain, but these peaceable animals are not territorial. Though males and females are both present in the same herds, you seldom see any overt signs of rivalry between the males. The herd is led by a big bull whose mastery appears to be unchallenged. However, you sometimes find aged eland bulls living by themselves; these must be displaced herd leaders driven out by younger and stronger rivals.

The Uganda kob is a classic example of the territorial animal. One's first impression of a kob herd is of animals unevenly scattered over the plain. Then you see that there are several distinct groups as well as a number of single animals. There is also a great deal of activity. While most of the kob graze or ruminate, others fight and chase each other; but they never cross the invisible line in the bush which demarcates the herd arena. The groups are the 'bachelor pools' comprised of up to a hundred males of any age from a few months upwards, and mixed herds of females escorted by one or two mature male kob. The single animals are the territorial males, the basis of an extremely complex society. Each one is master of his own little stamping ground, an area of twenty-five or thirty yards across; it includes a resting place where the kob sits and chews the cud, a defeating point and possibly an ant-hill on which he rubs his horns. Territories in the centre of the arena are of higher status than those on the perimeter.

Each kob territory-owner has emerged from a bachelor pool and once in possession he is constantly challenged. The aspiring bachelor makes threatening gestures which cannot be ignored; his horns are held forward and his ears stick out sideways. The frequent fights that result have the formality of fencing matches; the two animals keep their feet wide apart and their heads low as they battle away with interlocked horns. Ownership of territory gives some undoubted psychological advantage and the kob in possession nearly always wins. Indeed, a threatening gesture is often sufficient to drive away a rival. But competition is continuous; if a territorial kob chases off a rival or goes to a water hole to drink, he may well find that another has taken over in his absence.

The objective of territorial possession is to secure females for mating, and the constant fighting somehow produces sexual stimulation. Female kob are attracted to the territory where they immediately become the property of the owner. You then see the male strutting proudly around with small mincing steps and a strange stiff-legged gait. He lays his horns back upon his shoulders to indicate that he intends no harm, bares his teeth and points his nostrils to the sky giving a splendid exhibition of aggressive masculinity. He sniffs at the female's genitals and if she is in season the two animals mate. If not, she is usually chased to the limits of the arena. There is no breeding season. A female kob comes into heat as soon as her latest offspring is weaned, whereupon she leaves the female group to seek a territory-owner.

Dispossessed territorial males and unsuccessful challengers normally return to the bachelor pools where there appears to be little fighting, competition, or sexual activity other than spasmodic male to male mounting. An isolated individual may occasionally move right out of the arena. If a few females join him, and if there are no other kob about, they seem able to lead a normal family life without the complications of a territorial system. In the Uganda kob, according to Helmut Buechner, territoriality is an adaptation to environment.

This kob society is not static. Changes are always taking place in the relative situations of the individual animals. The arena, too, is changed from time to time as grazing requirements demand. Away from their territories the males forget their competition. They walk sedately in single file on their way to regular drinking places. To get to Lake George from one of the arenas in Queen Elizabeth Park, the kob have to cross a main road. They move to the verge and watch for passing cars. The leader springs lightly on to the tarmac. The others follow. But, after drinking, it becomes imperative for them to

Waterbuck: individual Waterbuck of opposite sex sometimes develop close associations

52

Impala: a charming domestic scene

get back to their territories as soon as possible.

Thomson's gazelle have a similar but looser organization and they develop harem herds at the time of greatest sexual activity. These are led by the old female who happens to be herd-sentinel at the time. She is not a permanent leader, as with red deer; but it is she who twitches her flanks to give the alarm signal and leads the herd in flight. The female gazelle is passive in courtship though she may run away if approached by an overpersistent male. If the male follows, the chase ends in mating; the male stands bolt upright with his forefeet touching the female's back.

The waterbuck also has a system of territories but these seem to embrace the male's whole living area and may be as much as a square mile in extent. The females wander between these territories, though individuals of opposite sex do sometimes appear to develop close associations. You may see a charming domestic scene of mother, father and calf; but, in fact, the bull's role is simply to wait for the female's next season and to make quite sure that he is in the right place at the right time for mating. When young waterbuck reach puberty, the males are driven away to form bachelor herds of their own. The young females stay with their mothers, however, and may do so for the rest of their lives, to produce permanent family groups within the herds. Fights develop when a visiting male wanders on to the territory of another and then responds to the challenge he invariably meets. I knew one waterbuck which kept the same territory for several years, defending this against the same challenger. The rivals seemed perfectly matched, but ownership of the territory did not change.

Wildebeest are territorial antelopes with a different system again. They are highly social animals and live in large herds. But, except in a few isolated localities, these herds are constantly on the move. Wildebeest territoriality is not related to a fixed area as in these other species. The bulls stay outside the breeding herds, defending their immediate surroundings wherever these may happen to be.

The great herds of topi that are sometimes to be seen come together for only part of the year when the males collect on the herd stamping ground, each individual owning a small territory which he defends in the usual way. The females and

Uganda Kob: the territorial male

OPPOSITE: Grant's Gazelle, mother and young

54

calves graze around the fringes of these territories and this is where mating takes place. After the rut has subsided, the herd splits up. The males keep to themselves; the pregnant females move off together in small parties. Eventually they drop their calves together, the young remaining with their mothers until the whole herd concentrates again.

Topi show a remarkable capacity to take up unusual formations and often succeed in giving the impression that they are being drilled. I once passed several hundred topi, all standing in line as though carefully 'dressed from the right'. They were facing towards me with their backs into torrential driving rain. Another time I was out with members of an African district council whom I was hoping to persuade that a certain stretch of country should be included in the Queen Elizabeth National Park. We were standing out in the open when a huge herd of topi came thundering past. They galloped along the line of astonished councillors like a regiment of cavalry at review. It was as if the topi themselves were demanding admission to the park.

Impala are not territorial. The males do not defend territories, nor do they deposit scent signals; but they become strongly attached to a home range and move only when they have to. Herds are of two main kinds: bachelor and harem herds. The bachelor impala are without a leader and, in spite of occasional mild striving for dominance, show little intolerance of each other. Competition between impala is largely limited to the struggle for possession of the females. There may sometimes be more than one male in a harem herd, but there is never more than one master-buck. He shepherds his females and urges stragglers to return if any should show signs of wandering; his technique is a sort of symbolized butting. If one of the females makes a serious attempt to desert, the master-buck usually follows her at full gallop.

The impala master-buck gains his harem in competition with other males. Young males are driven away from their mothers when they are ten or twelve months old; they then join a bachelor herd. Should a rival appear, the master usually demonstrates his superiority by attacking one of the young males which is still accompanying its mother. Only if this fails to impress will he go for the real rival. Differences are usually settled without an actual fight but what ultimately happens

The life of Impala is not all fighting

depends upon the status and level of individual aggressiveness of the rival animals – a male without a harem is always of inferior status. The first sign of conflict is one male circling another and making intimidating gestures with his horns. One or both may then show defiance by adopting a rigid, threatening posture with head up and hind legs apart, a stance commonly observed in many antelopes. If the lower ranking impala does not then run away, you see the other lift his tail, jump, shake his horns and possibly horn the ground. When the rivals are more or less equal, clashes can be violent: long, intense struggles with horns interlocked as the two impala thrust at each other. Damage is rarely serious, however.

Grant's Gazelle: comfort behaviour

Red Lechwe in Zambia

There is no rutting season in the Serengeti. The harem herd is a permanent feature of impala society. Courtship behaviour does not only lead up to mating, it assures tolerance of the male presence. The master-buck walks towards the female with his nose in the air, his neck stretched forward and his horns laid back. He makes an empty licking movement with his tongue. If the female is lying down, he paws and sniffs her rump; and he may walk round her with his tail fanned out to show off its white underside. Defecation and urination are not socially important to impala except when a female is in season. Then the master-buck will sniff and raise his head before going through the motions known as *flehmen*, already described in other antelopes. If competition for a particular female is strong, courtship activities are intensified, the master-buck standing up on his hind legs. Should an erring female wander too close to a bachelor herd, the master-buck may call attention to himself by moving to the centre of his harem and roaring or grunting with an audible exhalation of air through the nostrils. After a successful mating he usually indulges in a vigorous outburst of aggressive activity, snorting and roaring and lifting his tail before chasing another impala.

As with other antelopes, the life of the impala is not all courting and fighting. As well as feeding, resting, ruminating and taking salt, an appreciable amount of time is spent on comfort activities. Antelopes flick their ears and swish their tails when bothered by flies. They lick their flanks and backs, and sometimes even their feet, to clean themselves; they scratch their ears and their heads with the hoofs of their hind feet. When it rains, you sometimes see them lift and shake their legs. These are universal antelope preoccupations.

Indian blackbuck have much in common with impala. Behaviour is similar except for scent-marking habitually indulged in by blackbuck which mark trees in the same way as oribi. Aggressive males approach each other with a mincing gait, uttering short challenging grunts. Their horns lie back on their shoulders, and their facial glands are wide open. After a contest, the master-buck walks proudly round his females as if warning them to ignore his rivals. Sir Samuel Baker summed it up: 'The all-absorbing employment of the master-buck is to support his conjugal rights in a limited society of about twenty lovely females and five or six aspirants of various ages.'

OVERLEAF (LEFT): Rhinoceros puts a herd of Wildebeest to flight

OVERLEAF (RIGHT): Wildebeest and zebra on flooded grassland in the Ngorongoro Crater

CHAPTER FOUR

Antelopes and predators

Warthog share the grassland with the antelopes – Uganda Kob

OPPOSITE: Waterbuck and Egyptian geese in the Queen Elizabeth National Park

Left to themselves most antelope populations would increase by roughly twenty per cent each year. If there were no checks, numbers would double every four years and multiply tenfold in twenty-five years. In areas like the Serengeti there would very soon be nothing left for the antelopes to eat. Of course, this does not happen. Numerous predators prey upon the antelopes. This not only prevents overpopulation, it acts as a vital agency of natural selection. Predation is an essential part of the antelope story.

All animal life depends upon plant life for its supplies of energy. Only plants can change sunlight into food which can be eaten by animals. Consequently, as Professor Elton has explained, herbivorous animals are the basic class in animal society; they are usually preyed upon by the carnivores. This is the essence of Elton's 'food chain'. Among the larger mammals of Africa and the Asian steppes the antelopes are the main link in this chain. They are by no means the only herbivorous animals involved but they are the most numerous and the most widely distributed. Other herbivores such as elephants, hippopotamuses and rhinos are seldom preyed upon except by man; buffaloes are regularly killed by lions in some areas but the main check upon their numbers is through human hunting and disease. Giraffes are slow breeders and are not particularly numerous anywhere. Zebra and warthog share much of the African grasslands with the antelopes and are attacked by the same beasts of prey. But antelopes are preyed upon wherever they happen to live and they usually constitute a major part of the diet of several predators.

Silver-backed jackal and vultures feeding on a Wildebeest carcase

Elton uses the expression 'pyramid of numbers' in referring to the decrease in the number of individual animals involved at each stage of the food chain. In Africa, particularly, it is not always easy to express this in tidy mathematical terms. A pride of five lions usually kills a large antelope every three or four days or, say, a hundred antelopes a year. But the antelope population remains reasonably constant, indicating that the lions are feeding only upon the annual breeding increment. This means that a herd of five hundred antelopes is needed to support five lions. But leopards, wild dogs, and hyenas also prey upon the same antelopes, while a considerable part of any dead animal is actually eaten by vultures. And lions prey upon warthog, zebra, and buffalo as well as upon several species of antelope. They also range further afield than most of the herds upon which they prey. A rough balance is maintained, however. Predators breed, or at least rear their young, at a rate consistent with the food supply. If the antelope herds increase, it usually follows that the number of lions will also increase; so, in practice, will the frequency with which they kill. If the antelope herds decrease beyond a certain point, the lions move elsewhere; the effort of hunting has ceased to be worthwhile.

The Mweya peninsula (two square miles) in Queen Elizabeth Park used to support permanently twenty-one waterbuck, seventeen bushbuck, forty warthogs, twenty-one buffaloes and some elephants. A hundred hippos lived around the shores of the peninsula and grazed all over it at night. Five lions visited Mweya regularly, spending a few days there every three or four weeks. They usually made a kill: waterbuck, bushbuck, warthog, or occasionally a buffalo. As the hippos were eating all the grass and making conditions impossible we had to shoot them. The result was a dramatic improvement in the grazing. The number of waterbuck doubled in less than two years and had increased to seventy by 1964, six years after the shooting. There were comparable increases in the other animal populations and lions, instead of visiting the peninsula every few weeks, were present most of the time.

Before the shooting, there had been numerous hyenas which hunted in packs like gigantic hounds. Their main interest was the hippopotamus calves born in a patch of long grass scrupulously avoided by both waterbuck and buffaloes. The hyenas also killed other animals and rarely allowed a young waterbuck to live more than a few weeks. When the hippos were eliminated most of the hyenas went away, those that were left being primarily scavengers which task they carried out with horrifying efficiency. One night when lions killed a waterbuck near my house, I saw the five familiar lions and also ten or twelve hyenas, all fighting and squabbling over scraps. Next morning there was absolutely nothing left of that waterbuck.

Lions in Queen Elizabeth Park do not seem to show any particular preference among the animals upon which they prey, generally killing what they can most easily get. They often kill waterbuck, probably because of their size and the fact that they rarely change their home ground; they are also partial to topi and kob. Warthog is certainly one of their

OPPOSITE: Lioness passes a herd of Wildebeest: behaviour of antelopes when lions are not hunting

A troop of Oryx below the snows of Mount Kenya: Oryx are among the few antelopes to defend themselves against predators

67

specialities. It is also one they find difficult to kill as warthogs feed by day, spend the night below ground in old ant-bear holes and have extremely sharp tushes which they well know how to use. But lions, like most cats, are wilful individualists and generally feed as they feel inclined – I had two tame lions but could never persuade them to eat hippopotamus meat which is perfectly palatable.

Hunting by lions is probably not an entirely random business. Of course, they do not plan in advance or decide what prey to seek before setting out on a hunt: they move around their hunting territories and cover a wider range than most herbivores. They spend a few days in a kob area, then move to where they will find topi, waterbuck or perhaps buffaloes. A lion does not just chase after a herd of antelopes. It selects an individual victim which can be isolated from the herd. Only if this chosen prey-animal gets away will the lion turn its attention to another – this happens quite often, however, as there are times when lions show themselves to be surprisingly inefficient killers. They will certainly set whole herds into motion by roaring or giving them their scent. But before it can make a kill, a lion's intention and its aim must be exact. Again lions are opportunist and if an antelope chances to get too close to a hungry lion, the lion attacks; this is how many sick and aged antelopes end their lives.

In Nairobi Park, where kills have been recorded for several years, lions show a marked preference for wildebeest. Other prey-species include Grant's and Thomson's gazelles, impala, bushbuck, hartebeest, eland, zebra, and warthog: ostriches and giraffes are also present but these animals are not often killed by lions anywhere. Between 1954 and 1962 over 70 per cent of recorded lion-kills were wildebeest; and though wildebeest were the most numerous species, they accounted for only 35 per cent of the available ungulates. In 1962 a severe drought killed hundreds of antelopes and decimated the wildebeest population. The antelopes, in general, soon recovered from this disaster, but wildebeest were no longer the dominant species. By 1966 they had dropped to 6·4 per cent of the ungulate population. Nevertheless, in 1965, 30·7 per cent of the animals killed by lions were wildebeest; and in 1966, 26·5 per cent. In that year lions actually killed sixty-five wildebeest out of a total of less than 250, considerably more than the annual breeding increment. There are plenty of other suitable victims but the lions could be causing the local extinction of their most favoured prey.

Lions and certain other predators tend to kill male antelopes in their prime rather than females or immature animals – an analysis by Bruce Wright of records kept in several national parks revealed 60 per cent males among kills made by major predators. This may appear strange. Females are generally the more numerous, and the males would seem better able to defend themselves. But horns are not primarily weapons of defence and they may even make it easier for, say, a lion to concentrate and focus on an individual animal during the actual chase. Again, males guard the females and remain on the perimeters of the herds; they are liable to become solitary in old age; and the territorial male is always reluctant to leave his territory. So, on the whole, male antelopes are the more vulnerable.

Few antelopes make any serious attempt to defend themselves against beasts of prey which know well enough how to avoid their flailing hoofs. The oryx, sable and roan antelope, all of which use their horns in self-defence, are avoided by most predators if other prey is available. The main defences of most antelopes are speed and watchfulness, though some have developed strategems through which to confuse the enemy and avoid being taken by surprise.

In cover, a lion approaches a grazing herd with stealth, its belly close to the ground, moving only when it believes itself unobserved. Grazing antelopes, however, do not keep their heads down all the time. They look up and, if the danger is still unseen, you will see their ears turn slowly in the direction under suspicion. Then you may hear the alarm snort, or see an impatient tap of the foot or flick of the tail; or, in the case of gazelles, a twitch of the dark flank-band which can be made to produce a very obvious flash. But the ultimate reaction is hasty withdrawal to a safer distance: the 'flight-distance' which varies with the species and the circumstances.

Some antelopes rush away in a straight line; others dive for cover or curve and twist like coursed hares. Thomson's gazelle streak off with a 'hop, hop, hop' and a jump; then they start 'stotting', an action similar to the pronking of springbok. Impala jerk their heads, flick their tails and then dash away,

Uganda Kob: male antelopes are more vulnerable

Lions stalking Wildebeest: taking advantage of every bit of cover

jumping in all directions: this manoeuvre prevents the predator concentrating on an individual animal as it must to make a certain kill. Some antelopes appear resigned to their fate. I have seen a bushbuck stand on an ant-hill and allow a lion to kill it almost casually. Buffaloes better lions quite often. In the Queen Elizabeth Park, I once saw a magnificent maned lion running away from a buffalo with its tail between its legs and no greater dignity than an 'alley-cat'. But then this lion was enjoying a honeymoon. A lion and lioness had been mating in the grass, moving, playing and mating again. Absent-mindedly they drifted too close to some buffaloes and had to continue their love-making elsewhere. A herd of kob watched it all with apparent benevolence.

Lions hunt by night more often than during the day and employ various techniques. But the end of a successful hunt is always the same. The lion, or more usually the lioness, attacks diagonally from behind. After securing its prey with its claws, the lion bites for the throat or neck which may break as the antelope falls. It then goes for the victim's face; death by suffocation eventually follows. An experienced adult lion kills quickly. Youngsters may take twenty minutes or more to finish off a large antelope, and this is not a pleasant sight.

In the open a lion disdains stealth. You see it staring fixedly at a distant herd of, say, topi. The topi stare back but do not move as the danger is beyond their flight-distance. Then the lion's gaze fixes on a single male. Its tail swishes rhythmically from side to side. The crest of hair along its back is erect. It moves towards the distant antelopes: at first a purposeful walk, then a trot which becomes a canter as the distance

Lion carries off a Topi: an experienced adult lion

lessens. Only now does the topi turn to escape. But soon the lion is racing alongside. It springs. There is a scuffle as both lion and topi come down in the grass. The lion holds the head of its quarry between those massive paws as it bites for the throat. The topi herd soon settles down. Chasing, courting and other herd activities tend to be intensified after such an attack.

Lions often hunt as an integrated group or drive antelopes towards an ambushed member of the pride. Occasionally they wait in hiding near a water hole. When several lions are hunting together, one may run ahead to cut the selected victim out of a stampeding herd. The other lions follow, and the nearest brings the antelope down with a spring and a blow of its forepaw. The rest of the pride moves in. Sometimes you see one lioness charge forward after a lone antelope while another clamps her jaws onto the muzzle of the wretched creature. She twists the dying antelope onto its back to make sure of the final killing. But there is no fixed pattern. I once watched three lions hunt a single waterbuck in a different way again, taking advantage of every bit of cover they could find. In the Serengeti, not long ago, seventy dead wildebeests were found in a river. Tracks revealed that they had been stampeded by lions and had rushed headlong down a steep bank. Wildebeest seem particularly prone to this type of accident even at familiar fording places or where there is very little cover for possible enemies. Like most antelopes wildebeest almost always cross rivers as fast as they can.

Antelopes seem to know when lions are not on the hunt. They do not exactly ignore lions unless these are actually feeding or are obviously occupied in some other way; but the flight-distance is less and the antelopes react differently. They do not run away or start bounding about, but there is a nervous tension which you cannot miss. I recollect a day when the Ishasha plains in Queen Elizabeth Park carried a marvellous display of wildlife: chiefly kob and topi, in the usual dispositions of their kind, and distant herds of buffaloes. Three lions scrambled down from a fig tree in which they had been resting and walked across the antelope arena towards a river where they often used to drink. Some crested cranes took to the air and flew overhead calling their soulful, trumpeting calls. The kob and the topi stopped grazing. The territorial males turned and stiffened muscles to face the lions. The other

OPPOSITE: An Impala scratches its ear

73

Wildebeest and zebra at a watering place

antelopes watched suspiciously. Looking neither to right nor left, the lions wandered slowly on.

A study of over 200 kills in Nairobi National Park showed that six species of antelope had been preyed upon by ten species of predator. Thomson's gazelle suffered from all ten: lion, leopard, cheetah, hyena, wild dog, python, crocodile, baboon, jackal, and secretary bird, although the last four do not prey upon antelopes regularly. Fourteen impala were killed by seven of the predators, and seventy wildebeest by four. Lions and cheetahs each accounted for a Grant's gazelle. Lions killed three eland and three hartebeest.

In another study, covering several areas, it was found that cheetahs made use of twenty-five different prey-species but that most of their kills were either Thomson's or Grant's gazelles or impala. When they tackled any of the larger antelopes, they usually killed juveniles. Cheetahs, which are the fastest land animals on earth, hunt by sheer speed. They chase after their prey in the open, trip it or knock it off balance with a blow aimed at the hind legs, and then seize it by the throat. Cheetahs often prey upon such small antelopes as steinbok and oribi; and they used to be the traditional predator of the Indian blackbuck. But Indian cheetahs are now extinct, probably because their normal prey has been virtually wiped out by man whose cattle have usurped the grazing grounds. Tame cheetahs were kept for hunting blackbuck.

Leopards are the most secretive of the great cats. A short sharp dash, a spring from cover, or a leap from the branch of a tree is all that the victim knows. But leopards account for large numbers of small and medium-sized antelopes, particularly in the forests and denser woodlands where any number of forest duikers must be killed without anybody being any the wiser. The movements of a leopard at night can sometimes be followed entirely by sound: the chattering of monkeys, the occasional rasping grunt of the leopard itself and the bark which bushbuck make as they communicate their alarm to others of their kind. Leopards also take klipspringer from the rocky hills and kopjes as well as hyrax and baboons, and they often carry their kills up into the fork of a tree where a leopard can sometimes be seen with the remains of an antelope bigger than itself.

The smaller antelopes are preyed upon by several lesser predators such as the caracal and serval. Pythons feed mainly on rodents but also take small antelopes occasionally. The python waits beside a game trail and strikes at a passing duiker or bushbuck, sinking its teeth into the antelope's body. Pythons are not poisonous. They bite like dogs. As soon as a victim has been secured, the python coils around it, tightening up sufficiently to squeeze the breath from its body. Then the snake swallows the carcass whole. But pythons only feed about once a month and therefore have little effect on any antelope population. Secretary birds and certain eagles kill young antelopes at times. The remains are torn apart on the ground; even the most powerful eagle cannot take off when carrying anything heavier than a very young fawn. The magnificent crowned hawk eagle feeds largely on blue duikers and other small forest antelopes. The steinbok has learned to avoid such dangers by seeking safety in the old ant-bear holes it uses for breeding, though its normal reaction to danger is to lie flat on the ground.

Spotted hyenas play an important dual role, as scavengers and as major predators in their own right. As scavengers they sometimes drive lions away from a kill, thus forcing the lions to hunt again sooner than they would do otherwise. As direct predators, hyenas kill anything they can find. They are bold hunters, not cowards as is often suggested. But hyenas are not fighters; they attack what they can kill most easily which means that a majority of their victims are young or sick animals. They follow the seasonal migrations across the Serengeti plains, killing and eating any animal unlucky enough to fall by the wayside. They stay with the herds when calving takes place, and many new-born calves are among their victims. In fact, only the fittest survive to continue the evolutionary struggle.

Wild dogs (*Lycaon pictus*) are the most controversial of the killers. A few years ago most wardens shot them on sight on the grounds that they were cruel, wanton killers which created havoc among the antelope herds. But ideas change. As predators, wild dogs have a beneficial influence upon the various antelope species. They are no more wanton than other beasts of prey, and their greatest crime is probably that they hunt by day when you can see what they are doing. Like the wolf packs of the northern steppes, they need space in which to operate. You never find them in an unsuitable habitat; nor are they particularly numerous. Really large packs develop only under the most favourable feeding conditions. It seems that they then, however, lose their natural resistance to disease and become highly susceptible to distemper. Litters are large but comparatively few pups reach maturity.

Wild dogs may cause more immediate disturbance than other predators but this is not necessarily a bad thing. New breeding males take over the territories and the harems, and inbreeding is discouraged when the herds are broken up. Wild dogs, however, are a far-ranging species, so it is rare for them to influence any single antelope community for more than a short time. One day eight dogs appeared 'out of the blue' in one of the kob strongholds in Murchison Park. The

Hyenas killed this Wildebeest: their dual role

kob left but stayed away for only a few days. On another occasion, five wild dogs chased several hundred kob and hartebeest from an area of three square miles. The antelopes dashed off in a solid mass but settled down and resumed grazing in the usual way as soon as a kill had been made. When the dogs do establish themselves in a locality where prey is plentiful, you see them playing or chasing hares or just lying about with antelopes in the background, paying no more attention than they do to other predators.

Sometimes a scout dog goes out to locate possible prey; then you hear the eerie rallying call, 'oo-ah-oo', before the dogs begin to hunt. They hunt by sight, usually in the cool of the morning. Their own smell is too strong for them to be very sensitive to any scent left by a herd of antelopes. But this, together with a bell-like hooting, helps the dogs to keep in contact when on the move. There is a pack leader but no apparent hierarchy, and it is possible that different dogs take over the lead at different times. Once the hunt is on, however, the leadership does not change. Wild dogs have ample speed and endurance to run down any species of antelope.

First the antelope herd is set in motion. Then the lead-dog selects its prey and sets off in pursuit; the rest of the pack flanks out and follows. Discipline is rigid. The dogs nearly always stick to the selected prey-animal. At first the pace is slow. But the lead-dog increases its speed as the antelope begins to tire and soon catches up from behind. It bites for the belly or any extremity within reach; and the unfortunate antelope is eventually brought down by several dogs ripping and tearing at its entrails. Small buck are killed very quickly. Large antelopes take longer to die, but death is not necessarily slower or more painful than when it is the work of a lion or a leopard. Wild dogs are built for speed and endurance; they lack the special adaptations for efficient killing possessed by the big cats, notably their immensely powerful claws. Even so, wild dogs rarely have to hunt for more than ten minutes and usually kill more quickly than that.

John Goddard, a Canadian biologist, spent several months studying wild dog predation in the Ngorongoro crater. A pack of twenty-one dogs killed almost every day, but no more than was sufficient to provide each dog with six pounds of meat daily. When the dogs were not hunting, they appeared

Thomson's Gazelle: of the antelopes killed
60 per cent were Thomson's Gazelle

OPPOSITE : Bushbuck: stripes make an animal
difficult to see

amicable among themselves and antelopes readily approached
to within a hundred yards. Moreover, the dogs showed themselves to be the most efficient of the large predators. Almost
every hunt observed ended in a kill (86 per cent), and not a
single maimed or wounded animal was left to its fate. Of the
antelopes killed, 60 per cent were Thomson's gazelle, the
majority being territorial males. In every population of territorial antelopes there is likely to be a number of virile males
which are prohibited from breeding by their inability to secure
territories – in such species, the possession of a territory is a
prerequisite to securing a mate. The type of predation we are
now discussing has the effect of producing vacant territories
which are immediately taken over by vigorous young males at
the beginning of their breeding lives. This brings new blood
into the herds and is an example of one of the ways in which
predation may benefit a species.

Clearly, predation has a vital evolutionary function. Without the major predators, antelopes would not have evolved
into the superb beasts we know today. This concerns not only
eyesight, hearing, speed of movement and such behaviour as
the jumping of impala; colour and marking are equally involved. To bring off a kill, the predator has to aim not only
for an individual animal but also for a vital part of it, and this
usually has to be done when both are moving at speed.
'Countershading' is normal in antelope colouration. Most
antelopes are white or pale below and darker above. This is
difficult to see against the broken background of most land-
scapes – a single colour stands out much more clearly except
in the desert where it can be good camouflage. Stripes, bands
and blotches nearly always make an animal more difficult to
see; these are typical of most antelopes' coats as also are the
dark marks which disguise conspicuous features. All this
makes it much harder for a predator to achieve its objective.
It is, in fact, evident that in the process of evolutionary selection predators have tended to miss prey-animals in which
these characteristics were particularly well developed. In
Dr Hugh Cott's opinion: 'elaborate adaptations involving
colour, pattern, shape, and behaviour, and having every
appearance of design, could only be the result of some external
agent'. In the case of the antelopes the external agent must
have been the great beasts of prey.

CHAPTER FIVE

Survival and conservation

Antelopes act as hosts to numerous parasites and are subject
to various diseases. Most antelopes harbour ticks, chiefly at
the base of their ears or between their legs, and they are
subject to tick-borne diseases similar to East Coast fever in
cattle. Many antelopes are infested with lice though the
infestation seems to be heavy only when the animal is weakened
by injury or want. A few suffer from sarcoptic mange which is
often associated with the internal worms by which antelopes
are occasionally plagued: lung worms, bladder worms, intesti-
nal worms, and liver flukes. These do not appear to cause their
hosts much harm, although this is always difficult to assess as
most sick animals are killed by predators. Anthrax, recently
isolated in kudu and hartebeest but not yet in other species,
almost certainly causes a number of antelope deaths. But
antelopes are generally less susceptible to disease than domestic
livestock. They are undoubtedly more prone to natural cala-
mities, however, and many succumb during times of drought;
and, as some normally palatable grasses may become toxic
when weather conditions are abnormal, a few suffer from
plant-poisoning.

Rinderpest, a virulent eruptive fever which affects many
ungulates, reached tropical East Africa from Asia about 1890.
Thousands of cattle, buffaloes and antelopes died. The plague
spread to Sabi, now Kruger National Park, in 1896 and raged
for three years; it almost eliminated the buffaloes, eland,
kudu, roan, and some other antelopes. Since then outbreaks
have recurred and would have been equally catastrophic but
for modern veterinary techniques in relation to cattle and the

OPPOSITE: Addax: a desert antelope now
surviving in small numbers

81

Lechwe: most sick animals are killed by predators

natural resilience of antelopes. Survivors of an outbreak develop an immunity which is usually transmitted to their offspring.

Before the rinderpest, the African grasslands were generally better grazed than they are today, often by cattle and antelopes together. There was more forest but less scrub and thicket. By reducing the number of grazing animals, rinderpest encouraged thicket to encroach upon the grassland. And, as no species of tsetse fly can survive without shade, this allowed the fly to spread over wide areas not previously infested. Wild animals, among them a number of ungulates, are the natural food of the fly. They also harbour in their blood the various trypanosomes which the fly transmits to man or domestic animals. Certain trypanosomes cause sleeping sickness in man. Others produce an equally lethal cattle disease, known as *nagana* or *trypanosomiasis*, to which the wild animals have developed a natural immunity. Sleeping sickness is now under reasonable control, but a quarter of the land of Africa is denied to domestic stock by tsetse. Much of it is light sandy soil quite unsuited to intensive agriculture or cattle ranching. This is where the game animals generally live.

Elimination of the fly is obviously a major economic problem. But it is of vital importance only where soils are sufficiently rich to withstand the pressures of modern farming, a point which few governments have shown themselves willing to accept. Tsetse can be eliminated by killing the insects themselves, by removal of the shade or by removing the host-animals. Unfortunately this last method has been adopted in several African countries following the advice of Sir David Bruce who, in 1914 arrogantly recommended 'the early and complete blotting out of all wild animals in fly country'. The result has been a major threat to the survival of many antelope species without complete elimination of the fly.

It is easy enough to shoot out buffaloes and the larger antelopes, and this results in an immediate and spectacular reduction in tsetse numbers. But it is virtually impossible to shoot all the duikers, bushbuck, and bush pigs upon which the tsetse habitually feed. In spite of the slaughter, a few flies remain; the land is still not available to cattle. Shooting as a means of eliminating the tsetse fly is only intelligible if the land is immediately put to intensive human use. This rarely happens, even in those few areas which are capable of supporting such activity. This tragic policy of game destruction was first adopted in Rhodesia in 1919. Other countries followed suit, the policy becoming general after 1945. Countless thousands of antelopes have been killed, and the butchery still continues even though proved to be scientifically unsound as a method of controlling tsetse.

Except in a few areas, where the land is of high quality, antelopes are capable of using the African grasslands much more efficiently than cattle. This is not only in the way they graze, it is also that the biomass potential is higher. The right answer, in development terms, to much of the little used land of Africa is not substandard farming but the ranching of suitable species of antelope which are perfectly adapted to the conditions and are unharmed by tsetse. Antelopes, not oxen, are the natural cattle of Africa. Where there are no domestic cattle, the East African grasslands support over thirty tons live weight of wild ungulates to the square mile. Where cattle and wild ungulates share the land, the figure drops to fifteen tons. Where cattle graze alone the figure is as low as five tons though this can be increased to fifteen by careful husbandry. In the meat-hungry world of Africa, there is no justification for slaughtering thousands of antelopes to make land available for cattle.

The eland is the most obvious example of an antelope well suited to domestication; and the few eland farms already started show that this is a thoroughly practical proposition. These have been established in South Africa, Rhodesia and, with imported animals, in southern Russia. Eland thrive on poor soil and use a wide range of natural foods. Their temperament is docile, so that they make excellent draught animals. Eland cows have been milked successfully and have given up to twelve pints a day. Moreover, the carcase yields 10 per cent more meat than that of a bullock of the same body-weight; as with other antelopes, this is all good lean meat, whereas a bullock carries 28 per cent fat. Another antelope which immediately suggests itself for similar treatment is the wildebeest which probably converts more grass into flesh than any other herbivore. There can be little doubt that in Africa, except in the relatively few areas where the land is of high quality, antelopes can give a much higher return than cattle in terms of

Roan antelope at a watering place

Eland are well suited to domestication

calories and protein per acre. For several years ecologists, particularly Fraser Darling and Lee Talbot, have been arguing this approach to the problem of optimum use of the marginal lands of Africa.

The range of most antelopes is much as it was at the beginning of the century. But the overall density is greatly reduced and there are now wide gaps where distribution used to be continuous. Unfortunately the situation is getting worse, not better, and there is real threat to the survival of many species. Disease and tsetse-control hunting are by no means the only reasons for this. A number of factors, mostly man-made, are involved in this decline – man's influence is nearly always harmful to the conservation of natural fauna.

The human population is increasing steadily, so is the area under cultivation as the people take over more land for food and economic crops. Land in remote uninhabited regions is being opened up for development and by schemes for expanding human settlement. Where there is immediate competition between wildlife and the demands of domestic animals and agriculture, the wildlife invariably loses. This is the basic threat. When the wilderness is tamed, the natural habitats are destroyed; they may even be flooded by hydro-electric projects. No space is left for the wild animals. Then settlement cuts the migration routes and leaves animals isolated in small pockets. And even if they themselves can be protected, there may well be too small a population and too restricted an environment for long-term survival.

European settlement has invariably been accompanied by an all-out onslaught against the wildlife, notably in South Africa, Rhodesia, and the Kenya highlands. Huge numbers of antelopes have been killed quite indiscriminately to provide meat for farm and other labour. The immediate need was all that anybody thought about; nothing was left for the next generation.

On the whole, life was better organized in the old tribal Africa. The people fed on the wild antelopes, but hunting rarely involved killing more than a reasonable proportion of the herds – it must always have been wasteful, however, as there was no attempt to discriminate, and young animals and gravid females were killed without distinction. But today more people are ranged against fewer animals, often with firearms as well as spears, traps, bows and arrows. The old restraints and tribal disciplines are of less importance. Modern transport gives the hunters access to remote areas, and vehicles can now move about on the open plains almost as easily as the antelopes. Meat is a saleable commodity; commercial poaching has become the order of the day. All this is a major threat to the survival of the animals. Hunting for sport seldom does much harm provided that it is properly controlled and that 'bag' limitations are strictly obeyed.

The species which are in greatest danger are those whose range has always been most limited. The western giant eland, Lord Derby's nominate race, is now reduced to less than a hundred individuals in the interior of Guinea and the Ivory Coast. The Tora hartebeest, once common in the eastern Sudan, is now down to less than a thousand animals. The North African and Middle East gazelles survive only in a few pockets. There may be five hundred giant sable, mostly in Angola's Luando Reserve.

The swamp-dwelling lechwes have always enjoyed a restricted range: red lechwe chiefly on the Kafue floodplains and black lechwe only in the Bangweulu swamps. Even so, in 1900, there were reckoned to be a million black lechwe. By 1959 the population was down to 16,000; and, of these, only 4,000 now remain, putting this rare animal in serious danger of extinction. In 1932 there were an estimated 250,000 red lechwe on the Kafue flats. In 1959, following years of wasteful and unrestricted commercialized slaughter, the popu-

An unusual picture of a Bushbuck with its dorsal crest erected: the Bushbuck depends upon a well wooded habitat

lation was down to 30,000, a figure which has been more or less maintained during the past ten years. An occasional controlled hunt, or *chila*, is allowed: spearmen take part with their dogs, but firearms are now forbidden.

Some 12,000 of the surviving red lechwe live on the Lochinvar Ranch, two hundred square miles of grassy flood-plains which they share with wildebeest, oribi, zebra, lions and cheetahs. This has recently been bought by the Zambia government and is to become a permanent wildlife sanctuary, a most heartening move. Trials now being undertaken by the Zambian game department indicate that lechwe are admirable subjects for ranching. They are docile and gregarious and could probably be herded like reindeer. Given careful protection, it should be possible to build up a herd of 100,000 animals. An annual crop of up to 20 per cent would then yield a thousand tons of good lean meat, as well as hides and skins, for the needy people of Zambia. There is a secondary reason for conserving the lechwe: they fertilize the water with their droppings, as do hippos in many African lakes and rivers, and so help to convert vegetation into fish protein. Some readers may be horrified by such a mundane approach to conservation as ranching, but the basic idea is hardly new: the ancient Egyptians herded dorcas gazelle and possibly also addax.

Hunter's hartebeest, or hirola, which has been described as a hartebeest with the silky skin of a topi and the horns of an impala, has always been limited to a narrow range between the Tana and Juba rivers on the Kenya-Somalia border. The region is sparsely inhabited and was seldom visited by sportsmen. A few years ago this unusual antelope seemed to be thriving. Then the area was selected for a special development project to be financed by the United Nations, spelling certain doom to the antelope. Sportsmen flew in to secure a head while the going was still good. The only hope of saving the hirola lay in transferring the population, and a suitable site, well supplied with the grasses normally eaten by this antelope, was selected in Tsavo National Park. The hirola was easy enough to catch but proved to be unusually sensitive, several deaths occurring in the capture-pens – the cause was later discovered to be muscular dystrophy, a curable disease of cattle not previously isolated in a wild animal. Eventually in 1963, thirty hirola were moved by helicopter; they arrived in

The immaculate Lesser Kudu is finding conditions impossible

good condition and should form the nucleus of a breeding herd.

'Operation Oryx' received more publicity. The spectacular Arabian oryx, undoubtedly one of the rarest animals in the world, was being rapidly hounded to extinction by irresponsible hunting and human disturbance. In 1962, the Fauna Preservation Society mounted an expedition led by Ian Grimwood, and three of the few wild oryx still remaining in Arabia were caught in the Rub-al-khali desert. Since then a small breeding herd has gradually been collected. The oryx is now being established in Arizona and prospects seem good.

Outside national parks, reserves, and a few areas of untamable wilderness such as high mountain forests, the only hope of preserving antelopes in worthwhile numbers would seem to lie in game ranching of one kind or another. But this is only possible in relation to certain species: lechwe and eland, for example, as well as the saiga and Mongolian gazelle with which it is already practised. It is the function of national parks and reserves, however, to preserve all the different species. They are the ultimate reservoirs of wildlife.

Bohor Reedbuck

Some of these sanctuaries seem pitifully small for the task they have to perform. All require skilled and careful management to preserve a balanced inter-relationship between the various species and to preserve the habitat. Trees must continue to grow in the grassland, and scrub must not be allowed to encroach. If the habitat deteriorates, or even if it changes, the fauna will change too. An area intended to provide for one range of animals may end up with conditions suitable for quite a different range. When such situations occur, violent solutions may be required: these may include shooting to reduce certain animal populations, the control and use of fire, the provision of special protection for the vegetation in some areas and limiting access to water in others. These are examples of the kind of action that may have to be taken. Over-grazing by hippopotamuses in Queen Elizabeth National Park, and the action taken to restore the balance, has already been mentioned. Similar problems, caused by excessive concentrations of certain species, have arisen elsewhere. In my earlier book in this series, *The African Elephant*, I discussed the huge number of elephants now concentrated in the Tsavo National Park in Kenya and the damage that these animals are causing to the vegetation. Fire and elephants together are changing the natural scrub and woodland into grassland and steppe. Lesser kudu and other thornbush animals, including the rhinoceros, are finding conditions impossible; but zebra, oryx and the grazing antelopes generally are thriving and multiplying.

Many years ago the authorities of the Albert National Park in the Congo adopted a policy of complete non-interference with nature. The burning of grass is a major act of human interference, so grass fires were prevented. The grasslands became overgrown. The spectacular herds of topi or kob for which this park was famous thirty years ago are now no longer seen. But there are more elephants and more buffaloes.

These are examples of the kind of fundamental problem involved in the management of wildlife sanctuaries. If the antelopes and other animals are to survive for posterity these problems will have to be resolved. Primarily this is a matter for research. Each area and each species has its special problems. The present efforts in this direction, mostly financed from international funds, are extremely encouraging. Several research teams are in the field, notably the Nuffield Unit of Tropical Animal Ecology, based in Queen Elizabeth Park, and the internationally sponsored Serengeti Project which owes so much to the foresight and drive of Professor Bernhard Grzimek. Prospects are good. The new African governments, in many cases more sensitive to the demands of conservation than their colonial predecessors, seem to be realistic and far-sighted. But should these sanctuaries cease to exist, or should uncontrolled poaching allow them to deteriorate into nominal sanctuaries only, then the antelopes are doomed.

Poaching is a perennial problem to which the ultimate answer lies in education and improved living standards. In the short term, the need for police action is continuous. Few national park organizations or game departments have the resources to deal with this problem without help, particularly as most gangs of poachers are heavily armed and are usually quite prepared to use their spears against the rangers whose dangerous duty it is to combat their activities. And governments, whose responsibility for suppressing lawlessness is beyond dispute, are not always as actively co-operative as they might be. The poaching of rhinos and elephants, for horn and ivory, gets most of the publicity, but the majority of poaching forays are actually aimed at antelopes. And the majority of the animals caught in traps and snares are also antelopes.

The scientific argument for preserving wildlife is that it provides irreplaceable material for research into the evolution of natural flora and fauna. There is also a need to conserve variety and thus ensure against the ecological imbalance which can only result in erosion, or deterioration of the environment in some other direction, and is so easily produced by man's thoughtless actions. An all-out effort is required to safeguard 'the biological treasure-house of Africa's living present'. Fortunately the 'treasure-house' is also a unique tourist attraction, bringing millions of pounds into the countries where the wild animals live. This is the most telling of the economic arguments; tourism is a vital source of revenue.

Antelopes are the base of the wildlife pyramid. Without the antelopes the whole structure would collapse. There would be no tourist revenue and probably no possibility of ever making optimum economic use of the wild lands of Africa. In the last resort, however, it is the breath-taking beauty of these exquisite animals themselves that captivates us. I doubt if there is any finer sight than 'the processional frieze of antelopes' moving across the rippling grass and the wide horizons of the Serengeti. Man has created many superlative works of art; the antelopes are masterpieces in themselves.

> 'By valleys remote where the oribi plays
> Where the gnu, the gazelle and the hartebeest graze
> And the gemsbok and eland unhunted recline
> By the skirts of grey forests o'erhung with wild vine.'
>   (T. Pringle, 1789–1834)

Red Lechwe on the Lochinvar Ranch

Wildebeest at sunset

Appendix: Systematic List and Short Descriptive Notes

(The figures given immediately after the name indicate shoulder height and, when known, approximate weight of an adult male. Females are usually about 10 per cent smaller and lighter. Horn measurements, taken along the curve, are for well developed adult males. The various races, not listed, are liable to differ considerably in all these measurements.)

ORDER   ARTIODACTYLA   Even-toed Ungulates

FAMILY   BOVIDAE   Hollow-horned Ruminants

Subfamily TRAGELAPHINAE

Nyala   *Tragelaphus angasi*; 42 ins., 280 lbs.
   Male has shaggy grey-brown coat with white dorsal crest, flank-stripes and facial markings; fringe at throat; bushy tail. Female reddish. Open spiral horns in male only, 28–32 inches. (S.E. Africa)

Mountain Nyala   *Tragelaphus buxtoni*; 53 ins., 475 lbs.
   Smooth greyish-chestnut coat in both sexes; black and white crest; shorter and fewer white flank-stripes. Open spiral horns in male only, 34–46 inches. (Ethiopia)

Sitatunga   *Tragelaphus spekei*; 45 in. 220 lbs.
   Rough grey coat with white stripes and spots; long pointed and splayed-out hoofs. Horns, double-twisted with light tips, in male only, 22–35 inches. (W. Africa to Sudan and south to Zambesi)

Bushbuck   *Tragelaphus scriptus*; 30–36 ins., 100–120 lbs.
   Smooth chestnut coat with white flank-stripes, spots and face markings; large ears; bushy tail with white underside. Races vary considerably in size and colouring. Straightish, spirally twisted horns in male only, 12–20 inches. (Africa south of the Sahara)

Greater Kudu   *Tragelaphus strepsiceros*; 60–66 in. 650 lbs.
   Grey-brown coat and throat fringe; whitish dorsal crest, flank-stripes and chevron between eyes; large ears; short bushy tail. Magnificent open spiral horns in male only, 50–67 inches and up to 40 inches apart at tip. (S. Africa to Sudan and west to Lake Chad)

Lesser Kudu   *Tragelaphus imberbis*; 40 in. 230 lbs.
   Elegant miniature of last species without fringe; more numerous and distinct white markings. Horns, in male only, form closer spiral, 30–35 inches. (Ethiopia to Tanzania)

Eland   *Taurotragus oryx*; 69 ins., 1400 lbs.
   Fawn or tawny coat with whitish flank-stripes (absent in South Africa); large dewlap; long tufted tail; tuft of hair on forehead. Almost straight, smooth-textured and spirally twisted horns carried by both sexes but more slender in female, 28–40 inches. (Southern Sudan to S. Africa)

Lord Derby's or Giant Eland   *Taurotragus derbianus*; 69 ins., 1600 lbs.
   More impressive and massive than Eland. Rufous or sandy coat; flank-stripes more numerous and more obvious; heavier dewlap. Old bulls develop neck-mane. Spirally twisted horns with projecting ridges in both sexes, 35–47 inches. (West Africa to Congo-Uganda border)

Bongo   *Taurotragus eurycerus*; 48 ins., 500 lbs.
   Chestnut-red coat with vertical white stripes; white chevron between eyes and white marks on cheek; black underparts; large ears; long tufted tail. Open spiral horns, similar to Nyala, in both sexes, 30–39 inches. (Sierra Leone to Kenya)

Subfamily CEPHALOPHINAE

   All Duikers are squat animals with short straight horns, a tuft of hair on forehead and obvious facial glands.

Grey or Bush Duiker   *Sylvicapra grimmia*; 18–24 ins., 28 lbs.
   Grizzled coat; rather long ears; short tufted tail. Horns in male only, 4½–7 inches. (Africa south of the Sahara)

Peter's (Forest) Duiker   *Cephalophus callipygus*; 21 ins., 40 lbs.
   Yellow-brown and rufous coat; hair on nape directed forwards. Horns in male only, 3–5 inches. (W. Africa to Kenya)

Zanzibar (Forest) Duiker   *Cephalophus adersi*; 21 ins., 40 lbs.
   Almost indistinguishable from last species. (Zanzibar)

Bay (Forest) Duiker   *Cephalophus dorsalis*; 22 ins., 45 lbs.
   Bright bay coat with dark stripe along face and back; black patch on chest; black tail; short ears. Horns in male only, 2–3 inches. (W. Africa to Semliki and Angola)

Jentinck's (Forest) Duiker   *Cephalophus jentincki*; 32 ins., 100 lbs.
   Grizzled-grey coat; head, neck and chest-stripe almost black; white collar. Horns in male only, 4–5 inches. (Liberia)

Gaboon (Forest) Duiker   *Cephalophus leucogaster*; 22 ins., 45 lbs.
   Reddish-chestnut coat with dark stripe along back; white belly. Horns in male only, 3–5 inches. (Cameroons and Congo)

Red (Forest) Duiker   *Cephalophus natalensis*; 18 ins., 35 lbs.
   Foxy red coat; white tipped tail, short ears. Harvey's Duiker is a race of this species. Horns in both sexes, 3–4 inches. (Natal to Tanzania and Congo)

Black-fronted (Forest) Duiker   *Cephalophus nigrifrons*; 19 ins., 40 lbs.
   Distinguished from last species by slightly darker colouring, black blaze on face and elongated hoofs. Both are generally

known as 'Red Forest Duiker'. Horns in both sexes, 3 inches. (Cameroons to Ruwenzori and southern Congo)

Black (Forest) Duiker *Cephalophus niger*; 18 ins., 25 lbs.
Very dark blackish-brown coat with chestnut tuft; long narrow head. Horns in both sexes, 3–6 inches. (W. Africa)

Ogilby's (Forest) Duiker *Cephalophus ogilbyi*; 22 ins., 45 lbs.
Orange-red coat with black stripe along back. Horns in both sexes, 4 inches. (Fernando Po, Ghana to Cameroons)

Red-flanked (Forest) Duiker *Cephalophus rufilatus*; 14 ins., 28 lbs.
Reddish-buff coat with bluish-grey stripe up nose and along back; bluish-grey limbs; black crest. Stumpy horns in both sexes, 2–3 inches. (W. Africa to northern Congo)

Yellow-backed (Forest) Duiker *Cephalophus silvicultor*; 34 ins. 135 lbs.
The largest Duiker. Blackish-brown coat with large yellow patch extending from loins and rump to middle of back; yellow dorsal crest; white facial markings. Horns in both sexes, 5–8 inches. (Sierra Leone to Kenya and Zambia)

Abbot's (Forest) Duiker *Cephalophus spadix*; 27 ins., 120 lbs.
Chestnut-brown coat; grey face and throat; bright chestnut tuft and whitish tail. Horns in both sexes, 3–4 inches. (Kilimanjaro region)

Banded (Forest) Duiker *Cephalophus zebra*; 16 ins., 22 lbs.
'Zebra Antelope'. Reddish coat, cross-banded by twelve black stripes over back and down flanks. Horns in both sexes, 1–1½ inches. (West Africa)

Blue Duiker *Cephalophus (Guevei) monticola*; 14 ins., 12 lbs.
Slate-grey with some rufous on coat; rufous legs. Backward-sloping horns in both sexes, except in East Africa where females are hornless, 2–3½ inches. (Africa south of the Sahara)

Maxwell's Duiker *Cephalophus (Guevei) maxwelli*; 14 ins., 12 lbs.
Similar to Blue Duiker but mouse-grey coat with sepia face and back. Horns in both sexes, 1½–2½ inches. (West Africa)

Subfamily REDUNCINAE

Waterbuck *Kobus ellipsiprymnus*; 50 ins., 500 lbs.
Coarse, shaggy grey-brown coat; long hair on neck; small white patches and elliptical white ring on rump. Heavily ridged horns, in male only, sweep backwards and then curve forward at tip, 30–37 inches. (S. Africa to eastern Kenya)

Defassa Waterbuck *Kobus defassa*; 50 ins., 500 lbs.
Very similar to Waterbuck but rump entirely white; more 'noble' carriage. Horns in male only, 30–39 inches. (Zambia to Sudan and West Africa)

Kob *Kobus kob*; 35 ins., 200 lbs.
Red-gold coat with black and white markings, chiefly on face and legs, which vary according to race. Lyrate horns, S-shaped in profile, in male only, 20–28 inches. (Uganda, southern Sudan to Cameroons)

Puku *Kobus vardoni*; 36 ins., 150 lbs.
Reddish-yellow coat with some black markings; legs unmarked. Horns, in male only, similar to Kob but stouter, 18–21 inches. (Zambia and neighbouring parts of Tanzania and Congo)

Lechwe *Kobus leche*; 40 ins., 250 lbs.
Chestnut-red coat with some black and white on legs; rather long hair; elongated hoofs. Adult males in Black Lechwe race are blackish-brown. Horns, in male only, like Kob but more slender, 24–36 inches. (Zambia region)

Nile Lechwe *Kobus megaceros*; 38 ins., 200 lbs.
Rough blackish-brown coat, chestnut in females; white patches particularly on withers; white tail. Hoofs and horns as in Lechwe, 30–34 inches. (Sudan)

Reedbuck *Redunca arundinum*; 36 ins., 200 lbs.
Yellowish coat with dark leg stripes; short bushy tail; bare patch below ears. Horns, in male only, curve regularly forward, 15–17 inches. (S. Africa to southern Tanzania)

Bohor Reedbuck *Redunca redunca*; 28 ins., 100 lbs.
Coat almost uniformly fawn; bushy tail with white underside; bare patch below ears. Horns, in male only, hook forward at tip, 10–16 inches. (West Africa to Sudan and Tanzania)

Mountain Reedbuck *Redunca fulvorufula*; 28 ins., 60 lbs.
Greyish-fawn coat. Horns, in male only, curve forward as in Reedbuck, 6–9 inches. (S. Africa to Sudan)

Vaal Rhebok *Pelea capreolus*; 30 ins., 50 lbs.
Woolly greyish coat; long slender neck; long ears; slight build. Straight, upright horns in male only, 8–11 inches. (S. Africa)

Subfamily HIPPOTRAGINAE
All antelopes in this subfamily have fine sharp horns, carried by both sexes, long tufted tails and contrasting facial markings.

Roan Antelope *Hippotragus equinus*; 57 ins., 625 lbs.
Largest antelope after Elands. Coat fawn or grizzled; distinct dark and white facial markings; long tufted ears. Heavily ridged, backward-curving horns, 27–39 inches. (S. Africa to Sudan and West Africa)

Sable Antelope *Hippotragus niger*; 54 ins., 500 lbs.
Sleek, black or dark brown coat with white facial markings; long pointed ears; well developed mane. Scimitar-curved horns sweep backwards, 40–60 inches; up to 65 inches in Giant Sable of Angola. (S. Africa to Tanzania; isolated population near Kenya coast)

Oryx *Oryx gazella*; 48 ins., 450 lbs.
Light sandy coloured coat with dark markings; short dorsal mane. Gemsbok, Beisa, and Fringe-eared Oryx are races of this species. Straight, spear-like horns, 32–48 inches. (Kalahari to Ethiopia and Sudan but broken distribution)

Scimitar-horned or White Oryx *Oryx dammah*; 48 ins., 450 lbs.

Whitish coat with chestnut patches and almost black facial markings. Horns sweep backwards, 40–50 inches. (West of Lake Chad)

Arabian Oryx   *Oryx leucoryx*; 34 ins., 170 lbs.
Almost white with dark face, throat and leg markings; tail-tuft black. Slightly curved horns, 20–27 inches. (Arabia)

Addax   *Addax nasomaculatus*; 42 ins.
Rather heavy build; grey-white coat, darker in winter; hairy chestnut patch on forehead; broad flattened hoofs. Spirally twisted horns (three twists in male, two in female) 35–43 inches. (Sahara)

Subfamily ALCELAPHINAE
Large antelopes with high shoulders, long tufted tails and curved horns carried by both sexes.

Sassaby   *Damaliscus lunatus*; 48 ins., 350 lbs.
Chestnut-brown coat with black blaze on face, shoulders and legs. Half-moon shaped horns, 16–18 inches. (S. Africa to Zambia)

Topi   *Damaliscus korrigum*; 50 ins., 300 lbs.
Includes Tiang and Senegal Hartebeest. Sleek, red-brown coat with dark blaze on face, shoulders, and legs. Horns with single, slightly lyrate curve, 19–28 inches. (West Africa to Sudan and central Tanzania)

Blesbok   *Damaliscus dorcas*; 39 ins., 200 lbs.
Plum-coloured coat with white on rump, shoulders and face. Bontebok is slightly larger but lighter in colour and has smaller rump-patch. Horns similar to Topi, 15–20 inches. (S. Africa)

Hunter's Hartebeest   *Damaliscus hunteri*; 42 ins., 220 lbs.
Tawny coat with white chevron on forehead; face less elongated than true Hartebeests. Impala-like horns, 24–28 inches. (North-east Kenya)

Hartebeest   *Alcelaphus buselaphus*; 48–52 ins., 320–450 lbs.
Rufous, fawn or brown coat; very long face and very high shoulders. Angular horns rise from single pedicle on crown, 19–27 inches. Races include Jackson's and Lelwel, horns look V-shaped from front; Western with U-shaped horns; Red, Tora, and Coke's Hartebeests with horns like inverted brackets. (West Africa to Kenya and S. Africa)

Lichtenstein's Hartebeest   *Alcelaphus lichtensteini*; 48 ins., 300 lbs.
Tawny coat with rufous back and some black on face. Flattened horns curve inwards, 20–23 inches. (S. Africa to Tanzania)

Black Wildebeest   *Connochaetes gnou*; 46 ins., 360 lbs.
Also called White-tailed Gnu. Deep brown coat with black face, mane and beard. Horns curve forward like meat-hooks, 23–30 inches. (S. Africa)

Blue Wildebeest   *Connochaetes taurinus*; 50 ins., 550 lbs.
Also called Brindled Gnu. Includes White-bearded Wildebeest. Ox-like build; long, broad muzzle; throat-mane and beard; slate-grey coat with darker bands. Smooth, buffalo-like horns, 26–32 inches. (Kenya to S. Africa)

Subfamily NEOTRAGINAE
Klipspringer   *Oreotragus oreotragus*; 21 ins., 40 lbs.
Thickset, rough-coated, grizzled-brown antelope. Stands on tips of cylindrical hoofs. Straight horns, 4–6 inches, in both sexes in Masai race but otherwise in males only. (S. Africa to Ethiopia and Nigeria)

Oribi   *Ourebia ourebia*; 24 ins., 40 lbs.
Sleek, graceful fawn-coloured antelopes with bare black patch below ears, black-tipped tail. Haggard's Oribi (East Africa coast) greyer; some races lighter. Straight, upright horns in male only, 4–6 inches. (Africa south of the Sahara)

Grysbok   *Raphicerus melanotis*; 22 ins., 24 lbs.
Grizzled, reddish coat; large pointed, dark grey ears; short tail. Upright horns in male only, 3–4½ inches. (Coast of southern Africa)

Sharpe's Grysbok   *Raphicerus sharpei*; 20 ins., 24 lbs.
Tawny coat with white streaks; very large black-edged ears. Horns in male only, 1½–2 inches. (South Tanzania to Transvaal)

Steinbok   *Raphicerus campestris*; 22 ins., 30 lbs.
Sleek, red-brown coat; very large ears. Smooth straight horns in male only, 5–7 inches. (S. Africa to Kenya)

Suni   *Nesotragus moschatus*; 13 ins., 10 lbs.
Graceful little antelope with grey-brown coat, paler on throat and shoulders. Exudes musky odour. Livingstone's Suni is larger, 15 inches, and more rufous. Straight, ringed horns directed backwards, in males only, 2½–4 inches. (East Africa and east coast of southern Africa)

Royal Antelope   *Neotragus pygmaeus*; 10 ins., 8 lbs.
Smallest ruminant. Red-brown coat, paler on flanks; white lines along back and legs; tufted tail. Smooth horns in male only, 1–1½ inches. (West Africa)

Bates' Pigmy Antelope   *Neotragus batesi*; 13 ins., 15 lbs.
Slightly larger and darker than Royal Antelope but otherwise similar. Horns 1–1½ inches. (Equatorial forest, Cameroons to Semliki)

Phillips' Dikdik   *Madoqua phillipsi*;
Salt's Dikdik   *Madoqua saltiana*;   } 13 ins., 8 lbs.
Swayne's Dikdik   *Madoqua swaynei*;
Only minor colour differences in these Dikdiks. Coats greyish or grizzled with some rufous; pencil-thin legs; tuft of hair on crown; elongated snout. Spike-like horns in male only, 2–3½ inches. (All from Horn of Africa)

Kirk's Dikdik   *Madoqua (Rhynchotragus) kirkii*; 13 ins., 8 lbs.
Includes Damaraland Dikdik. Similar to above but snout

more elongated as in all *Rhynchotragus*; grizzled-grey coat with pale or rufous flanks. Horns in male only, 2–4 inches. (East Africa and South West Africa)

Guenther's Dikdik *Madoqua (Rhynchotragus) guentheri*; 15 ins., 9 lbs.

Like last species but slightly larger and snout even more elongated than in other Dikdiks; coat uniformly grey. Horns 2–3½ inches. (Southern Somali and northern Kenya)

Beira Antelope *Dorcatragus megalotis*; 22 ins., 20 lbs.

A large compact Dikdik with enormous ears but no elongation of snout; coat generally grey with white underparts and white eye-ring; large rounded hoofs. Horns, with slight forward curve, in males only, 4–5 inches. (Somali and Ethiopia)

Subfamily ANTILOPINAE

Blackbuck *Antilope cervicapra*; 32 ins., 85 lbs.

Coat uniformly brown, except for some white on face, becoming almost black in adult males; large expansile facial glands. Open corkscrew spiral horns in male only, 25–29 ins. (India and Pakistan)

Impala *Aepyceros melampus*
Black-faced Impala: *Aepyceros petersi* } 38 ins., 150 lbs.

Perhaps even more graceful than Blackbuck. Rufous-fawn coat, darker above; demarcation line on flank; white rump with black streak. Widespread lyrate horns in male only, 20–36 inches. (Kenya and Uganda to S. Africa)

Gerenuk *Litocranius walleri*; 38 ins., 115 lbs.

Rufous-fawn antelope with long legs and very long neck. Massive, heavily ridged lyrate horns in male only, 14–17 ins. (Tanzania to Ethiopia)

Dibatag *Amnodorcas clarkei*; 33 ins., 68 lbs.

Long-necked and long-tailed antelope with sandy-fawn coat; chestnut blaze on face. Horns, in male only, curve forward at tip, 10–12 inches. (Somali)

Springbok *Antidorcas marsupialis*; 30 ins., 75 lbs.

Cinnamon-brown coat with dark band above white underparts; when erected, fold of skin on back becomes a crest of white hairs. Lyrate horns in both sexes, 13–19 inches. (S. Africa)

Arabian Gazelle, Indian Gazelle *Gazella gazella*
Edmi or Cuvier's Gazelle *Gazella cuvieri* } 26 ins., 60 lbs.

Indian Gazelle is also called Chinkara. Rough, fawn to reddish coat; darker markings; no white on face; ill-defined flank-band. Horns with slight backward curve, in both sexes, 12–14 inches. (North Africa, Arabia, Middle East to India)

Dorcas Gazelle *Gazella dorcas*; 24 ins., 50 lbs.

Includes Pelzeln's Gazelle. Sandy-fawn coat with distinct black and white face markings; ill-defined flank-band; white rump; upper surface of tail black. Rather thick lyrate horns in both sexes, 10–15 inches. (Middle East and North Africa

to Somali)

Slender-horned Gazelle *Gazella leptoceros*; 28 ins., 65 lbs.

The Rhim Gazelle. Very pale sandy coat with faint flank and face markings; more white on face than Dorcas; large ears; long narrow hoofs; black-tipped·tail. Slender, heavily ridged and almost straight horns in both sexes, 14–16 inches. (North Africa and Arabia)

Speke's Gazelle *Gazella spekei*; 24 ins.

Coat very similar to last species; unusual thickening of nose. Horns similar to Dorcas, in both sexes, 11–12 inches. (North Somali)

Red-fronted Gazelle or Korin *Gazella rufifrons*; 26 ins., 60 lbs.

Includes Heuglin's Gazelle. Rather stocky build; sandy-red coat; white facial marking and black flank-band. Almost straight, heavily ridged horns in both sexes, 12–13 inches. (Senegal to Ethiopia)

Thomson's Gazelle *Gazella thomsoni*; 26 ins., 55 lbs.

Includes Mongalla Gazelle. Rufous coat with distinct black flank-band; white eye-streak; white on rump and black tail. Gently curving horns in both sexes, 15–17 inches. (Tanzania to Kenya and southern Sudan)

Dama or Addra Gazelle *Gazella dama*; 38 ins., 165 lbs.

The largest Gazelle. Very pale coat with some chestnut-brown on back and foreparts; no flank-band; rather long neck. Lyrate horns in both sexes, 14–16 inches. (Sahara and neighbouring regions)

Grant's Gazelle *Gazella granti*; 35 ins., 165 lbs.

Sandy-rufous coat with variable flank-stripe; white rump-patch bordered with black; chestnut, black and white facial markings. Splendid lyrate horns in both sexes, 22–31 inches. Horns of *robertsi* race (north-west Tanzania) have peculiar outward twist. (East Africa)

Soemmering's Gazelle *Gazella soemmeringi*; 34 ins., 100 lbs.

Similar to Grant's but less rufous and more white on coat. Horns turn inwards at tip, 14–23 inches. (Somali, Ethiopia and Sudan)

Persian Gazelle *Gazella subgutturosa*; 27 ins.

The Goitred Gazelle also called Black-tailed Antelope. Pale coat, paler on face, with dark eye-streak and white rump. Throat of male swollen during breeding season. Horns, in male only, divergent and slightly inward-curving at tip, 12–15 inches. (Persia to Turkestan and southern Gobi)

Tibetan Gazelle *Procapra picticaudata*; 25 ins., 45 lbs.

Procapra have shorter tails than *Gazella*. Pale coat with large white rump-patch. Slender horns, in male only, curve markedly backwards, 11–14 inches. Przewalski's Gazelle is fawn-coloured race with lyrate horns. (Tibet and north China)

Mongolian Gazelle *Procapra gutturosa*; 30 ins.

The Zeren, also called White Antelope. Pale fawn coat with white rump and light brown face; small ears. Light brown or grey horns, in both sexes, curve slightly backwards, 10–13 inches. (Mongolia)

Subfamily CAPRINAE
Tibetan Antelope   *Pantholops hodgsoni*; 32 ins., 110 lbs.
    The Chiru. Pale fawn-pink coat, densely woolly; face and part of limbs of male are dark brown. Nose swollen but not downward-curving. Almost straight black horns in male only, 23–27 inches. (Tibet)
Saiga Antelope   *Saiga tatarica*; 30 ins.
    Sturdy build. Coat dull yellow above and whitish below turns uniformly white and longer-haired in winter. Swollen nose with inflated nostrils directed downwards; short blunt ears. Amber coloured horns in male only, 11–14 inches. (Southern Russia, Caspian Sea to Gobi)

Subfamily BOSELAPHINAE (Status as Antelopes doubtful; closest affinities are with the *Tragelaphinae* and Buffaloes)
Nilghai or Blue Bull   *Boselaphus trayocamelus*; 54 ins.
    Ungainly, dark grey animal with mane and, in bull, tuft of hair at throat; females tawny; white patch on rump; long pointed head; forelegs longer than hind legs. Smooth upright horns in male only, 8–11 inches. (India)
Four-horned Antelope   *Tetracerus quadricornis*; 25 ins., 40 lbs.
    Dull brown coat with some lighter and darker markings; short legs. Two pairs of sharp straight horns in male only: front pair, sometimes absent, 2 inches; back pair, 3–5 inches. (India)

Note: African mammal systematics are under review. It has not, therefore, been possible to ensure that the arrangement of this list is fully up to date.

Select bibliography

Allen, G.M. (1939) *A Checklist of African Mammals* (Museum of Comparative Zoology, Harvard, U.S.A.)

Ansell, W.F.H. (1960) *Mammals of Northern Rhodesia* (Government Printer, Lusaka)

Bere, R.M. (1962) *The Wild Mammals of Uganda* (Longmans, London)

Bourlière, F. and Verschuren, J. (1960) *Ecologie des Ongules* (Institut des Parcs Nationaux du Congo, Bruxelles)

Brooks, A. C. (1959) *A Study of Thomson's Gazelle* (H.M.S.O., London)

Brown, Leslie (1965) *Africa, a Natural History* (Hamish Hamilton, London)

Burton, Maurice (1962) *Systematic Dictionary of Mammals of the World* (Museum Press, London); *University Dictionary of Mammals of the World* (Apollo Editions, New York)

Cloudsley-Thompson, J.L. (1965) *Animal Conflict and Adaptation* (Foulis, London); (Dufour Editions, Chester Springs, Pa.)

Darling, F.Fraser (1960) *Wildlife in an African Territory* (Oxford University Press)

Ellerman, J.R. and Morrison-Scott, T.C.S. (1951) *Checklist of Palaearctic and Indian Mammals 1758 to 1946* (Trustees of the British Museum (Natural History), London)

Hediger, H. (1951) *Psychologie Animale* (Institut des Parcs Nationaux du Congo, Bruxelles)

Hoier, R. (1950) *A Travers Plaines et Volcans au Parc National Albert* (Institut des Parcs Nationaux du Congo, Bruxelles)

Huxley, Julian S. (1964) *Essays of a Humanist* (Chatto and Windus, London); (Harper & Row, New York)

Maberly, C.T.Astley (1963) *The Game Animals of Southern Africa* (Nelson, Johannesburg); (Tri-Ocean Books, New York)

Maberly, C.T.Astley (1963) *Animals of Rhodesia* (Howard Timmins, Cape Town)

Morris, Desmond (1965) *The Mammals* (Hodder & Stoughton, London); (Harper & Row, New York)

Pitman, C.R.S. (1942) *A Game Warden Takes Stock* (Nisbet, London)

Roberts, Austin (1951) *The Mammals of South Africa* (Trustees of the 'Mammals of South Africa' Book Fund, Johannesburg)

Sidney, Jasmine (1965) *The Past and Present Distribution of Some African Ungulates* (Trans. Zool. Soc. Lond)

Ward, Rowland (1935 and 1962) *Records of Big Game* (Rowland Ward, London)

Williams, J.G. (1967) *A Field Guide to the National Parks of East Africa* (Collins, London)